COLORMYCODE

Jo Ann Smith

Illustrated by Elise Holm

 CyberSmith Publishing
Batavia, Illinois

ColorMyCode

Copyright@2019 by Jo Ann Smith

First Edition – August, 2019

This edition published August, 2019 by CyberSmith Publishing

Batavia, Illinois

ColorMyCode is available at special discounts when purchased in bulk for premiums and sales promotions as well as for fund-raising or educational use. For details, send email to sales@colormycode.com

Library of Congress Control Number: 2019908926

Smith, Jo Ann, author. | Holm, Elise, illustrator.

ColorMyCode / Jo Ann Smith ; illustrated by Elise Holm.

ISBN 978-1-7330471-0-4 (paperback)

Subjects: Computer programming. | Computer programming--Juvenile literature. | JavaScript (Computer program language) | JavaScript (Computer program language)--Juvenile literature.

Classification: DDC 005.133–dc23

Printed in the United States of America

Cover design by David L. Pedersen

Contents

A Note from the Author

Welcome to ColorMyCode!

This message is for parents, teachers, librarians and coaches. You don't have to know anything about computer programming to join with your child or learner as they progress through ColorMyCode. You can learn at the same time. It will be an exciting experience for everyone.

Above all — have fun!

Coloring is fun and so is coding!

JoAnn Smith

Before You Start

You should know how to:

- Turn on your computer.
- Use a mouse and a keyboard.

You Will Need:

- A computer, tablet or smart phone.
- The Chrome browser.
- An Internet connection.
- Colored pencils, gel pens, or crayons for coloring. Here are the colors you will need: Orange, Red, Blue, Gray, Purple, Green, Brown and Pink. (Do not use markers because the colors will "bleed" through to the next page making it unreadable.)

You Will See:

- It means this is something you can color. It is important to always color the JavaScript code when instructed. Coloring the code will help you learn JavaScript. You can color your code in the book, online at https://www.ColorMyCode.com or both. It is optional to color the drawings that you see, but it certainly will be fun to color them.
- An example of JavaScript code that has been colored is shown on the front cover. Check it out before you color your code for the first time.
- A How To video illustrating how to color in the book can be found at www.colormycode.com. Click on the Try It tab.
- A How To video illustrating how to color code online can be found at www.colormycode.com. Click on the Try It tab.
- Colored code for each of the hand colored exercises can be found at https://www.ColorMyCode.com/solutions. Check your coloring to be sure you have colored your code correctly. Online coloring is checked as you work.
- A How To video showing you how to correct your code if you make a mistake can be found at www.colormycode.com. Click on the Try It tab.
- Solutions for the "From Scratch" exercises can be found at https://www.ColorMyCode.com/solutions.
- Line numbers are included in some of the code examples that are not part of the code. They are included for reference only.
- JavaScript program code is shown in a different font. This is done to make the code stand out from the explanations.
- Keywords, variable names, operators, method names, special symbols are shown in a different font when used in the explanations.

You Should Find These Keys on your Keyboard:

Shift ⇧	Shift
Ctrl	Control
(9) 0	Shift + 9 and Shift + 0 – Open and Close Parentheses ()
+ =	Equal Sign (=)
" '	Shift + ' - Double Quotation Mark (")
: ;	Semicolon (;)
! 1	Shift + 1 – Exclamation Mark (!)
| \	Shift + \ - Pipe (|)
& 7	Shift + 7 – Ampersand (&)

You Will Learn More If You:

- Read the book in order. Each section builds on what you learned in earlier sections.
- Enter and run the JavaScript examples, then make changes to see what happens. Don't worry, I'll show you how to do this.
- Always enter and run the practice programs at the end of each section. Practice helps you learn.
- Always write your own "From Scratch" JavaScript programs as described at the end of each section.
- Always color your code and color one line of code at a time.

You are ready to begin. Have fun!

Acknowledgments

There are two truths I have become well aware of this past year. Turning an idea into a book is difficult. And, no one is successful without getting help from others. I had an idea but would not have been able to write this book based on my idea without the help of others.

I want to thank:

My husband Ray – who always tells me to go for it, no matter what I am up to. It helps to have a partner that encourages me to try new things.

My son Tim – for creating the online coloring world and for saying "You know mom, your idea for coloring code is a lot like diagramming a sentence and kids have been doing that for years". That was all I needed.

My 97 year old mom – for thinking that everything I do, or ever have done, is wonderful. Everyone needs a cheerleader like her.

My daughter-in-law Karla – for hatching my idea when we gave her the Anatomy and Physiology coloring book as a Christmas gift.

My grandson William – for giving me age-appropriate feedback as to what works and what doesn't work in my book.

Elise Holm – for creating the whimsical drawings that add so much fun to this book. And, for the opportunity to work with this wonderful young woman.

Martine Stuckey (Elise's Art Professor) – for sending Elise to me.

Marianne Fasano – for editing my book and making it a better version of itself. I appreciate her attention to detail and am happy to have gained a new friend.

David Pedersen – whose artwork graces the covers of my book. I am so impressed with his creative genius.

Batavia Public Library, especially

> George Scheetz (Library Director) – who is genuinely enthusiastic about my book.

> Joanne Zillman (Youth Services Manager) – who scheduled my Code For Kids classes that allowed me to trial the coloring techniques found in my book.

> Stacey Peterson (Adult Services Manager) – who helped me with ISBN numbers.

> Kerry Halter (Technical Services Manager) – who helped me with cataloging information for my book.

Everyone else whose positive words supported me. It kept me going.

Elise Holm – Illustrator

Elise is a devoted artist, musician, daughter, sister and aunt. She has grown up always looking for ways to satisfy her creative hunger. Elise studied Graphic Design at Illinois State University and Waubonsee Community College. She earned an Associate Degree and plans to make her way to Chicago in order to continue her education and seek creative opportunities.

Introduction

Your five senses are: sight, hearing, smell, taste, and touch. The senses are what you use to gain new knowledge. In this book, you will use sight and touch to help you learn how to program a computer. It'll be fun because you are going to use color (sight) and coloring (touch) to make it happen.

Did you know that using more than one of your senses helps you to learn easier and also helps you remember better? This old Chinese proverb shows the importance of the senses in learning.

I HEAR AND I FORGET

I SEE AND I REMEMBER

I DO AND I... understand

This is a RED LETTER day. A RED LETTER day is a special, happy and important day that you will always remember. Why is this a RED LETTER day? Because this is the day you are going to start learning how to program in JavaScript and at the same time, you get to color. Almost everyone likes to color.

A RED LETTER DAY!

What is JavaScript?

JavaScript is a programming language that lets you write computer programs. Lots of JavaScript programs are written to create web sites.

In addition to JavaScript, programmers who create web sites must also learn:

 AND

HTML is used to define what is on a web page.

CSS is used to describe how the items on a web page are arranged.

This book focuses on helping you learn JavaScript but will also show you how JavaScript works with HTML.

You should have a good reason to do something, especially something new.

Good Reasons To Learn JavaScript

1. Your browser has it, and you can do all sorts of things without buying anything or adding anything to your computer.

2. It's a very popular programming language.

3. It's everywhere. You'll find JavaScript in browsers like Firefox or Chrome. You'll find it on web pages including those with games. You'll even find JavaScript controlling robots.

4. JavaScript is easier to learn than other programming languages.

5. You can get a good job if you know how to program in JavaScript.

6. You can be a professional game developer if you know JavaScript well.

7. You can make your own blog. If you don't know what a blog is – Google It.

READY SET GO!

1. Install Chrome on your computer if it is not already there.
   http://www.google.com/chrome/

2. Open Chrome and then type about:blank in the address bar and press the Enter key. You should see a screen like the one shown.

This book uses the Chrome browser to write JavaScript code. These are the steps you should follow to use it on your computer.

This is the address bar where you type about:blank

Google

3. Open the JavaScript console. The JavaScript console is an area on your screen where you can type JavaScript commands. In Windows or Linux, you hold down the CTRL key and the SHIFT key and then type the J key, all at the same time. In the Mac OS, you hold down the COMMAND key and the OPTION key and then type J.

4. You should see the JavaScript console. Compare what you see on your screen to what you see below. Check to be sure you see a blank web page and a blinking cursor.

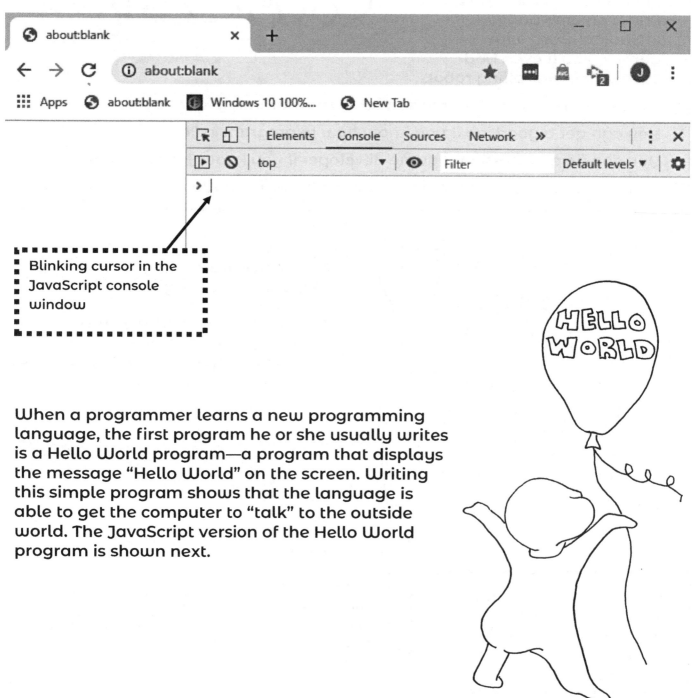

Blinking cursor in the JavaScript console window

When a programmer learns a new programming language, the first program he or she usually writes is a Hello World program—a program that displays the message "Hello World" on the screen. Writing this simple program shows that the language is able to get the computer to "talk" to the outside world. The JavaScript version of the Hello World program is shown next.

4

JavaScript programmers use a method called `console.log()` to display things on the console. A method is some code that performs a specific task. The `console.log` method is part of JavaScript. You can just use it without having to write any code. Console is just another word for your computer screen. Inside the parentheses you put the things you want displayed on the screen. In the Hello World example, you want the words Hello and World along with two exclamation marks to be displayed. Pay attention to the double quotes (" ") that surround the words Hello World!! The double quotes tell JavaScript that the characters inside the quotes make up a string. A string is a group of one or more characters.

Also, notice the semicolon (;) at the end of the statement. The semicolon in JavaScript is like a period in English. You put a period at the end of an English sentence to let the person reading your sentence know that this is the end. The semicolon at the end of a JavaScript statement tells the computer that this is the end of this statement.

1. Open the JavaScript console.

2. Type the code shown below after the blinking cursor.

    ```
    console.log("Hello World!!");
    ```

3. Check your typing. Be sure it is exactly the same as what you see in Step 2.

4. Press the Enter Key to run the program.

5. This is what you should see.

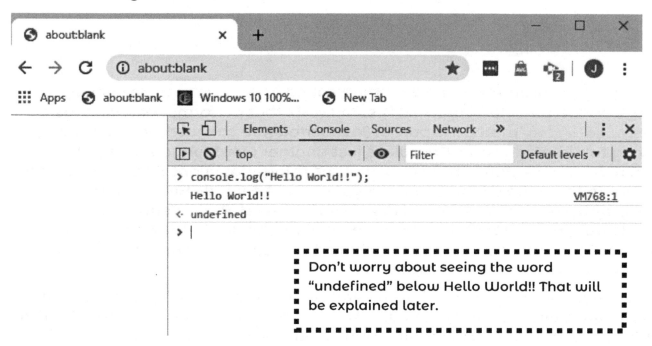

Don't worry about seeing the word "undefined" below Hello World!! That will be explained later.

6. JavaScript has displayed the string Hello World!! below the line that you typed. If you don't see this, you will see errors. Check and correct your typing and try again. Be sure that you have typed every letter and symbol correctly.

You just wrote your first JavaScript program!

When you write English sentences and paragraphs you have to follow the rules. For example, you place a period, an exclamation mark, or a question mark at the end of a sentence and you begin a sentence with a capital letter. It's also important to put a comma where it belongs. The rules are part of the syntax of English. If you don't follow the rules, your reader might not get the right meaning.

Let's eat Grandpa!

Let's eat, Grandpa!

If you don't believe this, you might end up eating Grandpa!

In JavaScript, syntax refers to the rules you must follow to write correct program statements.
If you don't follow the rules, the computer will not be able to understand what you want it to do.

In the Hello World!! program, you can see special symbols like parentheses ( ), double quotation marks " ", and a semicolon ;.

```
console.log("Hello World!!");
```

These symbols are part of JavaScript's syntax.
You will learn more about JavaScript's syntax as you continue in this book.

Color all the special symbols (parentheses, double quotes, semicolon) in the JavaScript statement above using the color orange. Color the method (console.log) using the pink color and color the string (Hello World!!) using the gray color.

You can also color this example on your mobile device using the QR code on the left or by visiting https://www.colormycode.com/colormycode/ex01.html

1. Open the JavaScript console.

2. Type the code shown below after the blinking cursor.

   ```
   console.log("I'm learning to program using JavaScript.");
   ```

3. Check your typing. Be sure it is exactly the same as what you see in Step 2.

4. Press the Enter Key to run the program.

5. You see that JavaScript has displayed the string

   ```
   I'm learning to program using JavaScript.
   ```

below the line that you typed. If you don't see this, you have typed something incorrectly. Check your typing and try again. Be sure that you have typed every letter and symbol as it is in Step 2.

 Color all the special symbols (parentheses, double quotes, semicolon) in the JavaScript statement below using the color orange. Color the method (console.log) using the pink color and color the string using the gray color.

```
console.log("I'm learning to program using JavaScript.");
```

You can also color this example on your mobile device using the QR code on the right or by visiting https://www.colormycode.com/colormycode/ex02.html

2

Practice Two

1. Open the JavaScript console.

2. Type the code below after the blinking cursor.

IMPORTANT! DO NOT PRESS the Enter key after each line. For programs that are more than one line of code, press SHIFT+ENTER to add another line. When all the lines are typed, press the ENTER key to run the program.

```
console.log("I'm hungry!");
console.log("I think I'll have a burger.");
```

3. Check your typing. Be sure it is exactly the same as what you see in Step 2.

4. Press the Enter Key to run the program.

5. This is what you should see.

```
I'm hungry!
I think I'll have a burger.
```

6. If you don't see this, you have typed something incorrectly. Check and correct your typing and try again. Be sure that you have typed every letter and symbol as shown in Step 2.

Color all the special symbols (parentheses, double quotes, semicolon) in the JavaScript statements below using the color orange. Color the methods (console.log) using the pink color and color the strings using the gray color.

```
console.log("I'm hungry!");
console.log("I think I'll have a burger.");
```

You can also color this example on your mobile device using the QR code on the left or by visiting https://www.colormycode.com/colormycode/ex03.html

Doing something "from scratch" means that you do it from the very beginning, without having some parts of it done for you. Here you are challenged to write your very first JavaScript program "from scratch."

Here is the description of the program.

Write a JavaScript program that displays two lines of text on the JavaScript console.

The first line is: `Learning JavaScript is fun!`
The second line is: `Soon, I'll be learning a lot more.`

There's a lot to learn in this section.

KEYWORDS

JavaScript considers some words to be special words. These words, called keywords, have a special meaning in JavaScript. In this section, you will use only one keyword and that word is `var`. You will use the `var` keyword to let JavaScript know that you want to create a variable.

From now on, use red to color keywords.

VARIABLES

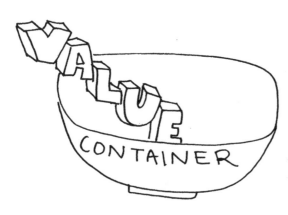

What does the word variable mean? Or maybe this is easier – what does the word vary mean? When you use it in an English sentence, it means "to change or something that changes". In JavaScript, variables are what a programmer uses to store values that their programs will need. Variables are containers. The values stored in variables can vary (change) as your program runs.

You will use blue to color variables.

Here Are Some Things To Know
About Variables

 Variables are containers that you can use to store data.

 Data is the information the computer will use when it runs your programs.

 The three different kinds of data in JavaScript that you will use are: numbers, strings, and booleans. More about this later in this section.

 In order to use a variable in a JavaScript program, you have to give it a name.

Giving Variables A Name

More rules! Here are the rules for giving variables a name in JavaScript.

- Variable names can contain letters, numbers, underscores (This is an underscore _), and dollar signs ($).

- Variable names must begin with a letter.

- Variable names are case sensitive. (Java Script knows the difference between uppercase and lowercase characters, e.g. `food` is not the same as `Food` or `FoOd` or `FOOD`.)

- Variable names cannot be keywords (like `var`).

Here are some variable names. Some of them follow the rules and some of them do NOT follow the rules: `my_name`, `numValue`, `3days`, `varValue`, `lastName`, `Cost`, `COST`.

 Find the variable names shown above that follow JavaScript's rules for naming variables and color them blue. Then, find the variable names that don't follow JavaScript's rules for naming variables and color them brown.

In JavaScript, variable names can be as long as you want. But you need to be careful here. Make your variable names just long enough to describe how they are going to be used, but not so long that they are hard to read or require too much typing. It's really easy to misspell the names of variables.

 It's pretty clear that a variable named `lastName` will contain someone's last name. The variable name `myFriendsLastName` is descriptive but too long and the variable name `ln` is too short and hard to understand.

Here's a funny term – Camel Case.

What do camels have to do with JavaScript? Nothing really, it's just a term used to describe something programmers use to make their variables easier to read.

Here's the problem – JavaScript variables cannot contain spaces which means that sometimes variable names will be hard to read.

Here is what programmers do – they start each variable name with a lowercase letter and then start all of the other words with a capital letter.

 `var lastName;`

Notice the word `last` starts with a lowercase letter and the word `Name` starts with a capital letter. This is Camel Case.

There are six different kinds of data in JavaScript. For now, you are going to use three of them. They are numbers, strings, and booleans.

Numbers are easy to understand. A number can be a whole number like someone's age (for example, 10) or the number of students in a class (for example, 24). A number can also be a fractional value like the price of an item (2.95) or a measurement (2.5 feet).

A string is a group of one or more characters, like a person's name. An example of a string is the last name "Smith" or a food type such as "burger".

The boolean data type in JavaScript represents one of two values: true or false. The word `true` and the word `false` are keywords in JavaScript. Now you know three keywords: `var`, `true` and `false`.

 What would be the data type of each of the following - number, string, or boolean?

Your age _____

How many brothers and sisters you have _____

The door is open_____

The price of an IPhone_____

Your mother's name _____

Your address _____

You are old enough to vote _____

The value of Pi _____

If you don't know the value of Pi—Google It.

Creating and Initializing Variables

Now that you understand the rules for naming a variable, you are ready to learn how to declare a variable. When you declare a variable, you are telling the computer that you are going to use the variable in your program.

This is how you declare a variable in JavaScript.

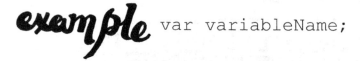

```
var variableName;
```

You can give a variable a value when you declare it. This is called initializing a variable. Here is an example.

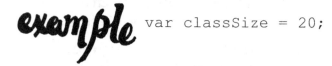

```
var classSize = 20;
```

You can also initialize variables with string values.

```
var menuItem = "Fries";
var homeCity = "Chicago";
```

Did you notice that there are double quotation marks at the beginning and end of strings? That's another rule. The rule is that you can use double or single quotes. In this book, let's use double quotes.

 Here is some JavaScript code that declares variables. Find the special symbols, keywords, variable names, numbers and strings, and use the chart to color what you find. Color the operator (=) using the green color. You'll be learning about operators in the next section.

 You can also color this example on your mobile device using the QR code on the left or by visiting http://www.colormycode.com/colormycode/ex04.html

Orange	Red	Blue	Gray	Purple	Green
Special Symbol	Keyword	Variable Name	String	Number	Operator

```
var feetInYard = 3;
var myShoeSize = 8;
var myHomeTown = "Batavia";
var daysInLeapYear = 366;
var myCatsName = "Mindre";
var catOwner = true;
```

There are only three types of statements that a programmer can use in a program. A programmer can use:

 Sequential Statements

 Selection Statements

 Iteration Statements

Let's start with sequential statements. Selection and Iteration statements will be explained later.

When a computer runs sequential statements that means your code will run in order, one line at a time beginning with statement 1, then statement 2, and so on until the end of your program is reached.

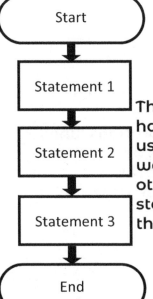

This is an easy section because all of the programs you have seen so far have used sequential statements. You use sequential statements in a program when you want the computer to perform actions one after the other. You can include any number of sequential statements in a program, but the statements must be in the correct order.

example This is a JavaScript program that uses sequential statements to display a famous children's poem.

```
1  var lineOne = "Mary had a little lamb,";
2  var lineTwo = "It's fleece was white as snow,";
3  var lineThree = "And everywhere that Mary went,";
4  var lineFour = "The lamb was sure to go.";
5  console.log(lineOne);
6  console.log(lineTwo);
7  console.log(lineThree);
8  console.log(lineFour);
```

This program is made up of four variable declarations (lines 1, 2, 3, and 4) and four sequential statements (lines 5, 6, 7, and 8) that execute one after the other. (The line numbers are not part of the JavaScript code. They are there for you to refer to as you read about the code.) When this program runs, this is what you see on the console (computer screen.)

```
Mary had a little lamb,
It's fleece was white as snow,
And everywhere that Mary went,
The lamb was sure to go.
```

 It's important in this program that you write the statements in the correct order and that they execute one after the other. Here is another example with the statements NOT in the correct order.

```
1  var lineOne = "Mary had a little lamb,";
2  var lineTwo = "It's fleece was white as snow,";
3  var lineThree = "And everywhere that Mary went,";
4  var lineFour = "The lamb was sure to go.";
5  console.log(lineTwo);
6  console.log(lineOne);
7  console.log(lineFour);
8  console.log(lineThree);
```

This program is made up of the same four variable declarations (lines 1, 2, 3, and 4) and four sequential statements (lines 5, 6, 7, and 8) that execute one after the other. Lines 1, 2, 3, and 4 are OK but the statements in lines 5, 6, 7, and 8 are NOT in the right order. When this program runs, this is what you see on the console.

```
It's fleece was white as snow,
Mary had a little lamb,
The lamb was sure to go.
And everywhere that Mary went,
```

You can see that the order of the statements makes a big difference.

The JavaScript code that follows declares variables and includes sequential statements. Find the special symbols, keywords, variable names, methods and strings, and color what you find. Color the operator (=) using the green color. You'll be learning about operators in the next section.

Orange	Red	Blue	Gray	Purple	Light Green	Pink
Special Symbol	Keyword	Variable Name	String	Number	Operator	Method

You can also color this example on your mobile device using the QR code on the right or by visiting http://www.colormycode.com/colormycode/ex05.html

```
var lineOne = "Mary had a little lamb,";
var lineTwo = "It's fleece was white as snow,";
var lineThree = "And everywhere that Mary went,";
var lineFour = "The lamb was sure to go.";
console.log(lineOne);
console.log(lineTwo);
console.log(lineThree);
console.log(lineFour);
```

Practice One

1. Open the JavaScript console.

2. Type the code shown below after the blinking cursor.

IMPORTANT! DO NOT PRESS the Enter key after each line. For programs that are more than one line of code, press SHIFT+ENTER to add another line. When all the lines are typed, press the ENTER key to run the program.

```
var name = "Jo Ann Smith";
var language = "JavaScript";
var message = "Hello World!";
console.log(message);
console.log(name + " is learning " + language + ".");
```

3. Check your typing. Be sure it is exactly the same as what you see in Step 2. For example, there is a space before the word, is, in the second `console.log` statement.

4. Press the Enter Key to run the program.

5. You should see

```
Hello World!
Jo Ann Smith is learning JavaScript.
```

below the line that you typed. If you don't see this, you have typed something incorrectly. Check and correct your typing and try again. Be sure that you have typed every letter and symbol as shown in Step 2.

6. Change the name to "Harry Potter" and the language to "Magic". Run the program again. Does the output change?

 In the JavaScript code below, find the special symbols, keywords, variable names, strings and methods, and color what you find. Color the operators (=) and (+) using the green color. You'll be learning about operators in the next section.

You can also color this example on your mobile device using the QR code on the right or by visiting https://www.colormycode.com/colormycode/ex06.html

Orange	Red	Blue	Gray	Purple	Light Green	Pink
Special Symbol	Keyword	Variable Name	String	Number	Operator	Method

```javascript
var name = "Jo Ann Smith";
var language = "JavaScript";
var message = "Hello World!";
console.log(message);
console.log(name + " is learning " + language + ".");
```

2

Practice Two

1. Open the JavaScript console.

2. You have learned that you are going to use three types of data in JavaScript – numbers, strings, and boolean. This JavaScript code lists the three types of data. Type the code shown below after the blinking cursor.

IMPORTANT! DO NOT PRESS the Enter key after each line. For programs that are more than one line of code, press SHIFT+ENTER to add another line. When all the lines are typed, press the ENTER key to run the program.

```javascript
var typeOne = "1. numbers";
var typeTwo = "2. strings";
var typeThree = "3. boolean";
console.log(typeOne);
console.log(typeTwo);
console.log(typeThree);
```

3. Check your typing. Be sure it is exactly the same as what you see in Step 2.

4. Press the Enter Key to run the program.

5. This is what you should see.

```
1. numbers
2. strings
3. boolean
```

6. If you don't see this, you have typed something incorrectly or your statements are not in the correct order. Check and correct your typing or put the statements in the correct order and try again. Be sure that you have typed every letter and symbol correctly.

 In the JavaScript code below, find the special symbols, keywords, variable names, strings and methods, and color what you find. Color the operator (=) using the green color. You'll be learning about operators in the next section.

You can also color this example on your mobile device using the QR code on the right or by visiting https://www.colormycode.com/colormycode/ex07.html

Orange	Red	Blue	Gray	Purple	Light Green	Pink
Special Symbol	Keyword	Variable Name	String	Number	Operator	Method

```
var typeOne = "1. numbers";
var typeTwo = "2. strings";
var typeThree = "3. boolean";
console.log(typeOne);
console.log(typeTwo);
console.log(typeThree);
```

Remember that doing something "from scratch" means that you do it from the very beginning, without having some parts of it done for you. Here is a challenge to write another JavaScript program "from scratch."

Write a JavaScript program that creates four variables that contain the four lines of the Happy Birthday song and then prints the words to the Happy Birthday song on the JavaScript console. Your program should print the words on four lines – like this.

```
Happy Birthday to You
Happy Birthday to You
Happy Birthday Dear (name)
Happy Birthday to You.
```

Replace (name) with anyone's name that you choose.

I have to think about it!!

Have you ever been told to think before you speak?

Have you ever been told to think before you act?

Now you are being asked to think before you code!

Why? To become a good programmer you will have to think before you begin to write your code. Flowcharts help programmers think about problems they are asked to solve.

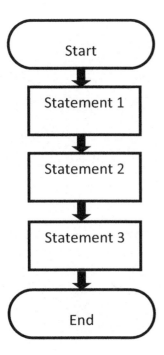

What is a flowchart? It's pretty simple. It's a diagram that is made up of symbols and arrows. Programmers use flowcharts to represent an algorithm.

Algorithm is a pretty big word. Relax, here's what it means. An algorithm is a step-by-step list of directions that need to be followed to solve a problem. You can think about it like solving a jigsaw puzzle. The puzzle pieces are the step-by-step list of directions. All of the puzzle pieces must be placed in the right place to finish the puzzle. The finished puzzle is the solution to the problem. Not too hard, right?

The programs you are writing at this point are easy. As you learn more about programming, you will be able to write more complicated programs. It's a good idea to get used to creating a flowchart, even for simple programs. Flowcharts help you organize your thoughts and that's a good thing.

Here are the symbols you need to know now. You will learn about other symbols as you continue to learn about JavaScript.

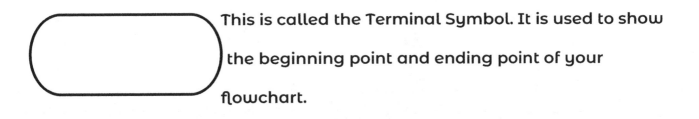 This is called the Terminal Symbol. It is used to show the beginning point and ending point of your flowchart.

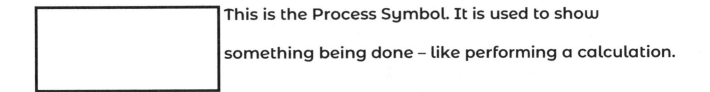 This is the Process Symbol. It is used to show something being done – like performing a calculation.

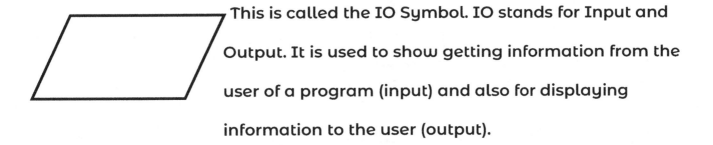 This is called the IO Symbol. IO stands for Input and Output. It is used to show getting information from the user of a program (input) and also for displaying information to the user (output).

 This is called the Flow Line Symbol. It is used to show the direction in which the flowchart moves.

PULLING IT ALL TOGETHER

Do you remember seeing this picture earlier in this book?

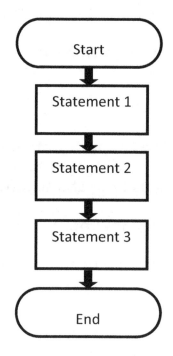

It's a flowchart. It has two Terminal Symbols (Start and End), four flow lines, and three Process Symbols. This flowchart shows that Statement 1 happens first, followed by Statement 2, and Statement 3.

Let's draw a flowchart to solve the following: Give instructions to a robot to stand up, turn around three times, and then sit down.

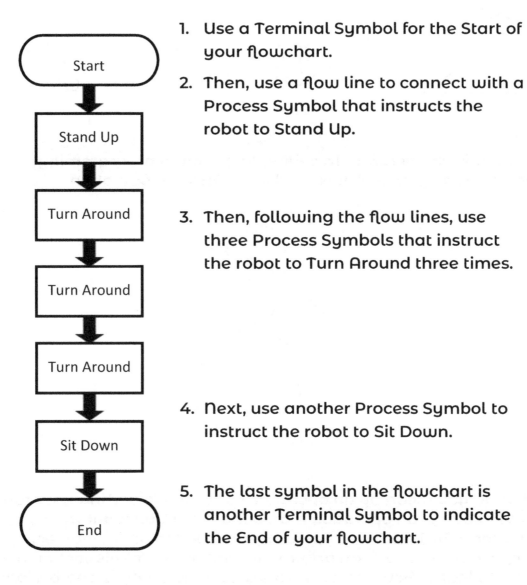

1. Use a Terminal Symbol for the Start of your flowchart.

2. Then, use a flow line to connect with a Process Symbol that instructs the robot to Stand Up.

3. Then, following the flow lines, use three Process Symbols that instruct the robot to Turn Around three times.

4. Next, use another Process Symbol to instruct the robot to Sit Down.

5. The last symbol in the flowchart is another Terminal Symbol to indicate the End of your flowchart.

As you continue on in this book, you will be using flowcharts to help you think about solutions to programming problems.

OPERATORS

So, what is an operator? In coding (also called programming), an operator is a symbol that is used to perform an operation.

What do you mean by an operation? Is that like getting your tonsils out? In coding, an operation is an action that you want the computer to perform. In JavaScript, operators are used to assign values, compare values, perform arithmetic, and more. In this section you are going to learn about the operators that assign values and perform arithmetic operations. You'll learn about other operators later.

ASSIGNMENT OPERATOR

You may not know this but you have already seen and used the assignment operator. It's the = (equal sign).

 Do you remember learning that you can give a variable a value when you declare it? This is called initializing a variable.

Here are some examples that you have seen in a previous section.

example
```
var feetInYard = 3;
var myHomeTown = "Batavia";
var daysInLeapYear = 366;
```

In each of these examples, you used the assignment operator (=) to give a variable its initial value.

In the JavaScript code above find the special symbols, keywords, variable names, numbers, strings, and operators, and use the chart to color what you find.

You can also color this example on your mobile device using the QR code on the right or by visiting https://www.colormycode.com/colormycode/ex08.html

Orange	Red	Blue	Gray	Purple	Light Green	Pink
Special Symbol	Keyword	Variable Name	String	Number	Operator	Method

example You can also use the assignment operator to change the value of a variable as your program runs.

```
1 var myAge = 10;
2 console.log("I am " + myAge + " years old.");
3 myAge = 11;
4 console.log("Next year I will be " +
                        myAge + " years old.");
```

On line 1 of this program, you create a variable named myAge and use the assignment operator (=) to give it an initial value of 10. You use the assignment operator again on line 3 where you change the value of myAge from 10 to 11.

When this code runs in the JavaScript console, this is the output of the program.

```
I am 10 years old.
Next year I will be 11 years old.
```

 In the JavaScript code on the previous page, find the special symbols, keywords, variable names, numbers, strings, operators and methods, and use the chart to color what you find. Color the operator (+) using the green color. You'll be learning about this operator later in this section.

 You can also color this example on your mobile device using the QR code on the left or by visiting https://www.colormycode.com/colormycode/ex09.html

Orange	Red	Blue	Gray	Purple	Light Green	Pink
Special Symbol	Keyword	Variable Name	String	Number	Operator	Method

ARITHMETIC OPERATORS

Arithmetic operators are the symbols you use in a JavaScript program to do arithmetic. You probably already know the arithmetic operators for addition (+) and subtraction (−). The multiplication operator is (*) and the division operator is (/).

You combine arithmetic operators and variables to create expressions. The computer evaluates the expression, and the result is what is called a value. Take a look at the JavaScript code shown next to see how this works.

```
1  var number1 = 5;
2  var number2 = 15;
3  var result;
4  result = number1 + number2;
5  console.log(number1 + " + "  + number2 + " is " + result);
```

On line 1 of this program you create a variable named number1 and assign it an initial value of 5 . On line 2 you create a variable named number2 and assign it an initial value of 15. On line 3 you create a variable named result but do not give it an initial value. Then, on line 4, you use the addition operator (+) to add the value of number1 (5) and the value of number2 (15), then use the assignment operator (=) to assign the sum (20) to the variable named result.

In the JavaScript code on the previous page, find the special symbols, keywords, variables names, numbers, strings, operators and methods, and use the chart to color what you find. Color the operator (+) using the green color. You'll be learning about this operator later in this section.

You can also color this example on your mobile device using the QR code on the right or by visiting https://www.colormycode.com/colormycode/ex10.html

Orange	Red	Blue	Gray	Purple	Light Green	Pink
Special Symbol	Keyword	Variable Name	String	Number	Operator	Method

Did you get that? Here's a picture to help you understand this better.

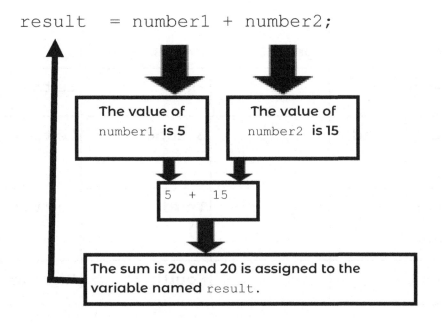

```
result  = number1 + number2;
```

The value of number1 **is 5**

The value of number2 **is 15**

5 + 15

The sum is 20 and 20 is assigned to the variable named result.

When you write code that includes operators, you need to pay attention to the order in which more than one operation is performed. This is called the precedence of operations. Here's how it works. Each operator is assigned a certain level of precedence.

 For example, multiplication has a higher level of precedence than addition. So in the expression

8 + 3 * 5,

the 3 * 5 would be multiplied first. When the multiplication is done, then the 8 is added. The result is the value 23.

 What happens when two operators have the same precedence? There are rules for that, called the rules of associativity. These rules determine the order in which operations are done when more than one operator with the same precedence are included in a statement.

Here is a table that shows the precedence and associativity of the assignment and arithmetic operators that you have learned.

Operator Name	Operator Symbol	Order of Precedence	Associativity
Parentheses	( )	First	Left to right
Multiplication and Division	* /	Second	Left to right
Addition and Subtraction	+ −	Third	Left to right
Assignment	=	Fourth	Right to left

34

Here is an example. In the statement,

example   result = 4 + 8 - 5;

the addition and subtraction operators have the same precedence. As shown in the table on the previous page, the addition and subtraction operators have left-to-right associativity, which means the statement will be evaluated from left to right (4 + 8 is added first; then 5 is subtracted).

Here is a picture that helps you understand how precedence and associativity works.

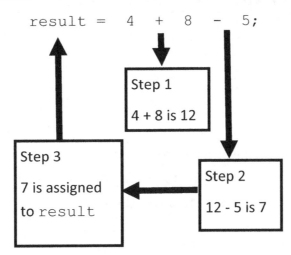

result =   4   +   8   -   5;

Step 1

4 + 8 is 12

Step 3

7 is assigned

to result

Step 2

12 - 5 is 7

There is an operator in the table that you have not seen before. It is the parentheses operator ( ). The parentheses operator has the highest precedence. Use this operator to change the order in which operations are performed.

example average = quiz1 + quiz2 / 2;

This statement is incorrect. It is supposed to find the average of two quiz scores by adding the two quiz scores, then dividing by 2 (the number of test scores). The way this statement is written, the computer will first divide the value in the quiz2 variable by 2, then add it to the value in the quiz1 variable because the division operator has a higher precedence than the addition operator.

For example, if the value of `quiz1` is 86 and the value of `quiz2` is 96, the value assigned to `average` is 134 (96/2 is 48 and 48 + 86 is 134). This is not the correct average of these two test scores. But if you use the parentheses operator in this example, you can make the addition occur before the division.

Here is the correct statement.

```
average = (quiz1 + quiz2) / 2;
```

In this example, the value of `quiz1`, 86, is added to the value of `quiz2`, 96 (86 + 96 is 182), then the sum is divided by 2 (182 / 2 is 91). The value assigned to `average`, 91, is the correct result.

After the arithmetic is done, the result, 91, is assigned to the variable `average`.

Can you figure out why this is true? If you answered that the assignment operator has lower precedence that is correct. The assignment operator has lower precedence than the arithmetic operators.

CONCATENTION OPERATOR

You have seen the concatenation operator many times already but it has not been explained to you yet. The concatenation operator (+) is used to combine two or more strings into one longer string. Or, you can think of concatenating strings as "adding" them together to create one string.

You might want to combine the strings "JavaScript" and "Programmer" to make the new string "JavaScript Programmer."

You use the + operator to combine these strings.

```
var newString;
newString = "JavaScript" + " " + "Programmer";
```

 Did you notice the " " between the "JavaScript" string and the "Programmer" string in the previous example? The " " string contains a space. It is included to provide a space between the string "JavaScript " and the string "Programmer". When these three strings are concatenated, there will be a space between them.

As you know, the + symbol is also used as the addition operator in JavaScript. If you use the + with numbers it will add the two numbers; if you use the same operator with two strings, it will concatenate (combine into one) two or more strings.

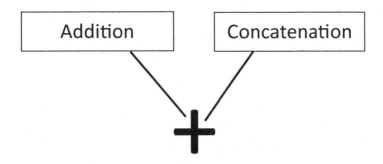

1. Open the JavaScript console.

2. Type the code shown below after the blinking cursor.

DO NOT PRESS the Enter key after each line. For programs that are more than one line of code, press SHIFT+ENTER to add another line. When all the lines are typed, press the ENTER key to run the program.

```
var num1 = 12;
var num2 = 6;
var num3 = 18;
var answer1, answer2, answer3;
var answer4, answer5, answer6;
answer1 = num1 * num2 + num3;
answer2 = num1 * (num2 + num3);
answer3 = num1 + num2 - num3;
answer4 = num1 + (num2 - num3);
answer5 = num1 + num2 * num3;
answer6 = num3/num2;
console.log("Answer 1: " + answer1);
console.log("Answer 2: " + answer2);
console.log("Answer 3: " + answer3);
console.log("Answer 4: " + answer4);
console.log("Answer 5: " + answer5);
console.log("Answer 6: " + answer6);
```

38

3. Check your typing. Be sure it is exactly the same as what you see in Step 2.

4. Press the Enter key to run the program.

5. This is what you should see when you run the program.

```
Answer 1: 90
Answer 2: 288
Answer 3: 0
Answer 4: 0
Answer 5: 120
Answer 6: 3
```

6. If you don't see this, you have typed something incorrectly or your statements are not in the correct order. Check and correct your typing and try again. Be sure that you have typed every letter and symbol correctly.

In the JavaScript code below, find the special symbols, keywords, variable names, numbers, strings, operators and methods, and use the chart to color what you find.

You can also color this example on your mobile device using the QR code on the right or by visiting https://www.colormycode.com/colormycode/ex11.html

Orange	Red	Blue	Gray	Purple	Light Green	Pink
Special Symbol	Keyword	Variable Name	String	Number	Operator	Method

```javascript
var xBox = 12;
var nintendo = 14;
var ps4 = 10;
var total;
total = xBox + nintendo + ps4;
console.log("I have " + xBox + " xBox games");
console.log("I have " + nintendo + " Nintendo games");
console.log("I have " + ps4 + " PS4 games");
console.log("I have a total of " + total + " games");
```

2

Practice Number

1. Open the JavaScript console.

2. Remember flowcharts? Here is a flowchart for a program that converts a Fahrenheit temperature to Celsius.

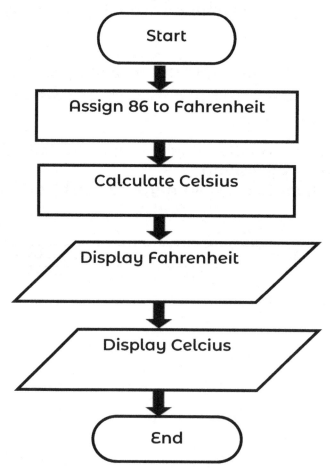

3 Here is the JavaScript code that was written using the steps listed in the flowchart to convert a Fahrenheit temperature to a Celsius temperature.

4 Type the code shown next after the blinking cursor.

DO NOT PRESS the Enter key after each line. For programs that are more than one line of code, press SHIFT+ENTER to add another line. When all the lines are typed, press the ENTER key to run the program.

```javascript
var fahrenheit = 86;

var celsius;

celsius = (fahrenheit - 32.0) * (5.0 / 9.0);

console.log("Fahrenheit temperature: " + fahrenheit);

console.log("Celsius temperature: " + celsius);
```

5. Check your typing. Be sure it is exactly the same as what you see in Step 4.

6. Press the Enter key to run the program.

7. This is what you should see when you run the program.

```
Fahrenheit temperature: 86

Celsius temperature: 30
```

7. If you don't see this, you have typed something incorrectly or your statements are not in the correct order. Check and correct your typing and try again. Be sure that you have typed every letter and symbol correctly.

 In the JavaScript code shown next, find the special symbols, keywords, variable names, numbers, strings, operators and methods, and use the chart to color what you find.

You can also color this example on your mobile device using the QR code on the right or by visiting https://www.colormycode.com/colormycode/ex12.html

Orange	Red	Blue	Gray	Purple	Light Green	Pink
Special Symbol	Keyword	Variable Name	String	Number	Operator	Method

```javascript
var fahrenheit = 86;

var celsius;

celsius = (fahrenheit - 32.0) * (5.0 / 9.0);

console.log("Fahrenheit tempterature: " + fahrenheit);

console.log("Celsius temperature: " + celsius);
```

3

1   Open the JavaScript console.

2   Type the code shown below after the blinking cursor. This code finds the area and perimeter of a rectangle.

DO NOT PRESS the Enter key after each line. For programs that are more than one line of code, press SHIFT+ENTER to add another line. When all the lines are typed, press the ENTER key to run the program.

```
var length = 12;
var width = 5;
var perimeter;
var area;
perimeter = 2 * (length + width);
area = length * width;
console.log("The length is: " + length);
console.log("The width is: " + width);
console.log("The perimeter is: " + perimeter);
console.log("The area is: " + area);
```

3. Check your typing. Be sure it is exactly the same as what you see in Step 2.

4. Press the Enter Key to run the program.

5. This is what you should see below the lines that you typed. If you don't see this, you have typed something incorrectly. Check and correct your typing and try again. Be sure that you have typed every letter and symbol correctly.

```
The length is: 12
The width is: 5
The perimeter is: 34
The area is: 60
```

6. Change the length to 5 and the width to 6. Run the program again. Does the output change? If you do not include the parentheses in this statement— `perimeter = 2 * (length + width);` — what would happen?

42

It's time for another challenge to write a JavaScript program "from scratch."

Here is the description of the program. Write a JavaScript program that displays the days of the week along with the high temperature for each day. Then, display the average temperature for the week.

Here is a list of the high temperatures recorded for one week.

Monday	78 degrees
Tuesday	81 degrees
Wednesday	85 degrees
Thursday	65 degrees
Friday	75 degrees
Saturday	77 degrees
Sunday	80 degrees

HERE TO HELP

Here's a hint. You find the average by adding the numbers, then dividing the sum by the number of items added.

Before you begin to write your code, draw a flowchart here.

I have to think about it!!

Soon you are going to learn how to write JavaScript programs that can make decisions. That means you need to know what kind of symbol to use in your flowcharts to show a decision must be made.

Here is the new symbol.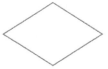

It's called the Decision Symbol. Usually, a Yes/No question or a True/False question is asked. Depending on the answer, your program will follow flow lines that indicate which path your program should take.

PULLING IT ALL TOGETHER

Let's draw a flowchart to solve the following: You need to write a program that can figure out if a number is an even number. That is, can it be divided by 2? You think about this problem for a while and figure out that all you have to do is divide the number by 2, and if there is no remainder (the remainder is 0), then it's an even number. Easy, right??

But, how can you do this in a program? Here's some good news. There is a JavaScript operator that is just what you need. It's called the Modulus Operator. Sometimes the Modulus Operator is called the Remainder Operator. The symbol for the Modulus Operator is % (percent sign). The Modulus Operator performs division and finds the remainder.

Here's how it works. Take a look at this code.

```
1  var myAge = 11;
2  var remainder;
3  remainder = myAge % 2;
```

In this code, on line 1 the value of myAge is initialized with the value 11. On line 3, you see the modulus operator (%) being used like this, remainder = myAge % 2;. This causes the computer to divide the value of myAge (11) by 2 and then find the remainder. In this example, when 11 is divided by 2, the remainder is 1 and this value is assigned to the variable named remainder. **Right?**

Aha! Now, you know that 11 is not an even number because the value of remainder is not 0.

Now that you have seen how to use the modulus operator, let's draw a flowchart to solve the Even Number problem.

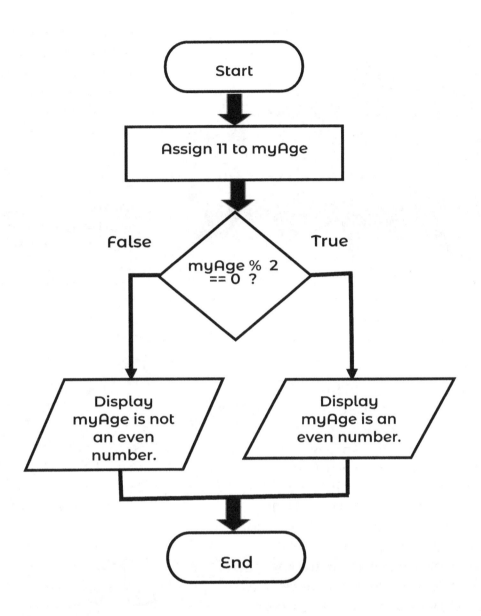

What do you do if you want the user of your program to give you some information? Maybe you want to know their name or their favorite sport or their favorite color. You can do this by using interactive input statements, which are statements that ask, or prompt, the user to enter the information.

Here's the good news! There is an easy way to do this in JavaScript. It's called the `prompt()` method. Do you remember methods? In JavaScript, a method is some code that is written to perform a task. Usually it is a task that is done often. In JavaScript, some methods are already written for you. All you need to do is use it. That's right, you don't have to write the code. The `prompt()` method is one of those methods that JavaScript just gives you.

Think of it as a gift from the folks who created the JavaScript programming language.

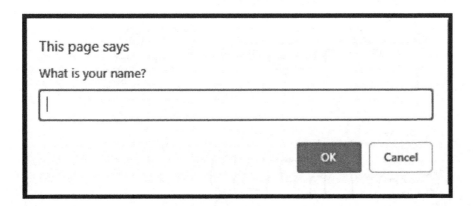

Open the JavaScript console and type the following statement.

```
var name = prompt("What is your name?");
```

Press the Enter key.

You should see a pop-up window that asks you "What is your name?" along with an empty text box and two buttons, OK and Cancel.

Now you can type your name in the text box and then click the OK button. When you have done this, the pop-up window will disappear and the value that you typed in the text box is assigned to the variable called name.

```
var name = prompt("What is your name?");
```

 Did you notice that the string "What is your name?" is placed within the open and close parentheses? And, did you notice that this is what appears on the pop-up window?

```
var name = prompt("What is your name?");
```

 Did you recognize this as an assignment statement? Do you see the assignment operator (=) ?

To prove that the `name` **variable contains the name you typed in the prompt pop-up window, type the following in the JavaScript console, then run the program.**

```
var name = prompt("What is your name?");

console.log("Your name is " + name);
```

You should see your name displayed.

 Do you want to try another method? This one is for output. Its name is `alert()` **and it is often used when you want to display some information to the user of your program. The information pops up in a window on the screen along with an OK button that must be clicked for the program to continue.**

Open the JavaScript console and type the following statements.

```
var name = prompt("What is your name?");
alert("Your name is " + name);
```

Press the Enter key to run the program.

This is what you should see:

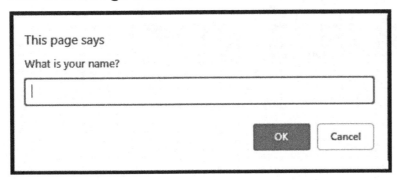

Type your name in the text box and then click the OK button. When you have done this, the prompt pop-up window should disappear and the alert pop-up window should be displayed as shown.

Click the OK button and the program should end.

 In the JavaScript code that follows, find the special symbols, keywords, variable names, strings, operators and methods, and use the chart to color what you find.

You can also color this example on your mobile device using the QR code on the right or by visiting https://www.colormycode.com/colormycode/ex13.html

Orange	Red	Blue	Gray	Light Green	Pink
Special Symbol	Keyword	Variable Name	String	Operator	Method

```
var name = prompt("What is your name?");
alert("Your name is " + name);
```

RIDDLES

Here is a riddle for you.

When is a number not a number?

Let's look at the following JavaScript code to figure out the answer.

```
var num1;
var num2;
var answer;
num1 = prompt("Enter first number: ");
num2 = prompt("Enter second number: ");
answer = num1 + num2;
alert(num1 + " + "  + num2 + " is " +  answer);
```

It looks like you have declared three variables: num1, num2 and answer. And it looks like you are asking the user of your program to enter two numbers using the prompt() method. Then you add them and store the results of the addition in the variable named answer. Finally, you use the alert() method to display the arithmetic problem and the answer. Pretty easy, right? NOT!

If you run this JavaScript program, here is what you should see.

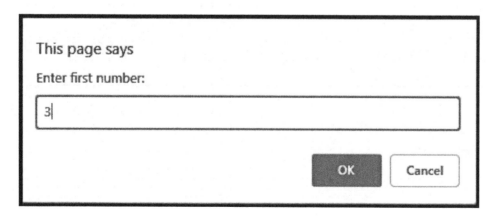

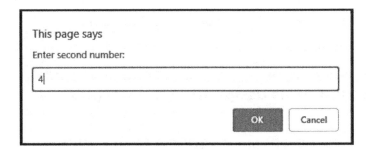

This page says

Enter second number:

4|

OK   Cancel

This page says

3 +4 is 34

OK

GENIUS AT WORK to

What? You don't have to be a math genius know that 3 + 4 is 7 – NOT 34. So what happened?

There are two things to know here. First, do you remember that the + operator can be used to add numbers but it can also be used to add strings? When adding strings, the + is called the concatenation operator. Second, what if you were told that when you use the `prompt()` method, it thinks everything entered in the pop-up window is a string. In other words, everything entered is a character or a group of characters.

When this line of code executes

```
num1 = prompt("Enter first number: ");
```

a pop up window is displayed and the user enters the number 3. When the user clicks the OK button, the computer gets the 3 and assigns it to the variable named `num1`. But – it didn't get the number 3, it got the string "3". Do you notice the double quotes? That means what is inside the quotes is a string.

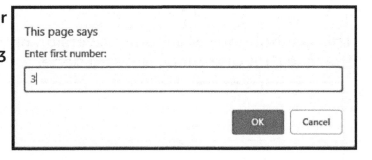

This page says

Enter first number:

3|

OK   Cancel

The same thing happens when this line of JavaScript code runs.

```
num2 = prompt("Enter second number: ");
```

A pop-up window is shown on the computer screen, the user enters 4, clicks the OK button and the string "4" is assigned to the variable named num2.

When this line of code runs, the value of num1 is added to the value of num2.

```
answer = num1 + num2;
```

But, because num1 and num2 contain strings, num2 is concatenated to num1 and that ends up being 34.

 What can you do to make this code do addition, not concatenation?

Here's the answer. You can use Number(). Number() is another method the JavaScript developers have given you. It changes a string to a number. Here's how you use it. You put the string you want to change to a number within the parentheses following the word Number, like this, Number(num1) and Number(num2). Doing this causes the + operator to work with numbers. Now addition is done and 3 + 4 is 7.

Here is the program written using Number().

```
var num1;
var num2;
var answer;
num1 = prompt("Enter first number: ");
num2 = prompt("Enter second number: ");
answer = Number(num1) + Number(num2);
alert(num1 + " + "  + num2 + " is " +  answer);
```

This is what you see when this version of the program runs, 3 + 4 = 7. You see that arithmetic is being done.

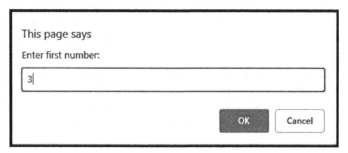

This page says

Enter second number:

4

OK   Cancel

This page says

3 +4 is 7

OK

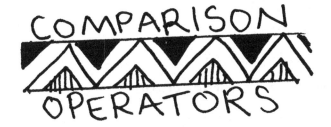

COMPARISON OPERATORS

Soon, you are going to start writing JavaScript programs that can make decisions. Before you can do that, you have to learn a few more JavaScript operators. These are the comparison operators and – you guessed it – they are used to compare things in your programs.

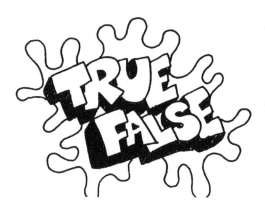

When you use a comparison operator, you can ask a question that results in a true or false answer. Depending on the answer, your program will execute different statements that perform different actions.

Here are the comparison operators and how they are used in JavaScript programs.

Comparison operators can be used to see if a value is:

==	equal to another value
>	greater than another value
<	less than another value
!=	not equal to another value
>=	greater than or equal to another value
<=	less than or equal to another value.

Let's see if you can figure out how comparison operators are used. First take a look at the two variables that are declared and given initial values.

```
var value1 = 12;
var value2 = 25;
```

Now, let's see if you can determine if the following expressions are true or false. Color the word True using a green color or False using a red color next to the expressions that follow.

value1 < value2	True or False
value1 <= value2	True or False
value1 > value2	True or False
value1 >= value2	True or False
value1 == value2	True or False
value1 != value2	True or False

Do you remember what precedence and associativity mean? You learned what they mean when you learned how to use the assignment and arithmetic operators (= , +, −, *, /).

Precedence refers to the order in which more than one operation is performed. Associativity determines the order in which operations are done when two or more operators have the same precedence and are included in a statement.

Here is a new table that shows the precedence and associativity of the assignment, arithmetic and comparison operators. The Modulus operator has been added to the chart. It has the same precedence and associativity as multiplication and division.

Operator Name	Operator Symbol	Order of Precedence	Associativity
Parentheses	( )	First	Left to right
Multiplication, Division and Modulus	* / %	Second	Left to right
Addition and Subtraction	+ −	Third	Left to right
Comparison	> < >= <=	Fourth	Left to right
Equality	== !=	Fifth	Left to right
Assignment	=	Sixth	Right to left

 Remember that you can change the order of precedence by using parentheses.

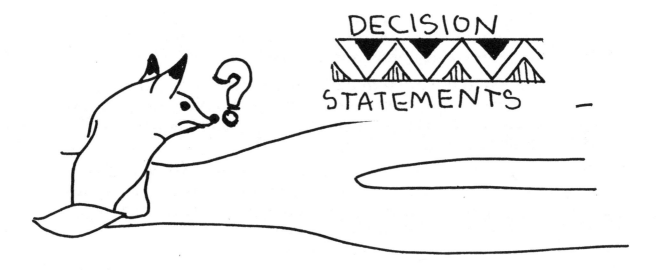

In a program, every decision depends on whether an expression evaluates to true or false. You can use decision statements to change the order in which statements are executed. Decision statements are sometimes called branching statements, because they cause the computer to make a decision, and then choose one or more branches (or paths) in the program.

There are different types of decision statements in JavaScript. Let's get started with one that is called the if statement.

The if statement is a single-path decision statement which means if an expression evaluates to true, your program executes one or more statements, but if the expression evaluates to false, your program will not execute these statements. There is only one path—the one your program takes if the expression evaluates to true. In either case, the statement following the if statement is executed.

Let's take a look at the syntax, or rules, for writing an `if` statement in JavaScript.

```
if(expression)
    statementA;
```

You begin with the keyword `if`.

 Do you remember that a keyword is a word that has a special meaning for JavaScript? What other keywords have you already learned about? If you answered `var`, `true` and `false`, you're right.

After you type the keyword `if` to begin an `if` statement, you follow it with an expression placed within parentheses.

When an `if` statement is included in a program, the expression within the parentheses is evaluated. If it is true, then the computer executes `statementA`. If the expression in parentheses is false, then the computer does not execute `statementA`.

 Remember that whether the expression evaluates to true and executes `statementA`, or the expression evaluates to false and does not execute `statementA`, the statement following the `if` statement executes next.

Here's something new and really important. A JavaScript statement, such as an if statement, can be either a simple statement or a block statement.

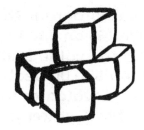

A block statement is made up of more than one JavaScript statement. To make a block statement in JavaScript you have to put the statements (one or more) inside a pair of special symbols called curly braces.

This is what curly braces look like.   { }

If you want your program to run more than one statement as part of your `if` statement, you must put those statements inside a pair of curly braces.

 If you don't do this you are in for some bad news! What's the bad news? Only one statement will execute. It's possible that this is what you want to happen but, usually it will cause problems.

 Here's an example of a program that uses curly braces correctly. Let's call it the Grandma Discount program. Your grandma wants to buy a new smart phone. She has asked you to find out if she can get a discount because she is a senior citizen. You find out that seniors can get $20.00 off the price if they are at least 59 years old. Your grandma is 63. Here is a program that illustrates an `if` statement that uses the comparison operator (<) to test if the value of the variable `grandmaAge` is less than 59. The program also uses a block statement. You can see the first curly brace in line 4 and the second curly brace in line 7.

```
1    var grandmaAge = 63;
2    var seniorDeal = 20.00;
3    if(grandmaAge < 59)
4    {
5        seniorDeal = 0.00;
6        console.log("Sorry no senior deal for you.");
7    }
8    console.log("Senior Deal : " + seniorDeal);
```

In this program, the variable named `grandmaAge` is initialized to the value 63 on line 1 and the variable named `seniorDeal` is initialized with the value 20.00 on line 2 . Your program is written to assume that a $20.00 deal is available. On line 3, the comparison `grandmaAge < 59`, evaluates to false and the block statement does not execute. The block statement (lines 4 through 7) is made up of the two statements within the curly braces: `seniorDeal = 0.00;` and `console.log("Sorry no senior deal for you.");`

Because the expression evaluates to false, the block statement does not execute. Whether the expression evaluates to true or false, the next statement to execute is the following output statement shown on line 8.

```
console.log("Senior Deal : " + seniorDeal);
```

Open the JavaScript console, type the grandma discount program, then run it. This is what you should see when you run the program.

```
Senior Deal : 20.00
```

Now, change the value of grandmaAge to 53 and run the program again. This is what you should see.

```
Sorry no senior deal for you.
Senior Deal : 0.00
```

In the Grandma Discount program that follows, find the special symbols, keywords, variable names, strings, numbers , operators and methods , then use the chart to color what you find.

You can also color this example on your mobile device using the QR code on the right or by visiting https://www.colormycode.com/colormycode/ex14.html

Orange	Red	Blue	Gray	Light Green	Purple	Pink
Special Symbol	Keyword	Variable Name	String	Operator	Number	Method

```
var grandmaAge = 63;
var seniorDeal = 20.00;
if(grandmaAge < 59)
{
    seniorDeal = 0.00;
    console.log("Sorry no senior deal for you.");
}
console.log("Senior Deal : " + seniorDeal);
```

61

Notice that there is not a semicolon at the end of the line with the `if` and the expression to be tested. Including a semicolon at the end of this line is allowed, but it could create a logic error in your program.

A logic error causes your program to produce incorrect results. In JavaScript, the semicolon (;) is called the null statement and is considered a statement that is allowed in JavaScript. The null statement is a statement that does nothing. Take a really good look at this BAD example. It's a little difficult but really important to understand how the null statement works.

```
1  var grandmaAge = 63;
2  var seniorDeal = 20.00;
3  if(grandmaAge < 59);
4  {
5      seniorDeal = 0.00;
6      console.log("Sorry no senior deal for you.");
7  }
8  console.log("Senior Deal : " + seniorDeal);
```

If you write an `if` statement as shown above, your program will test the expression `grandmaAge < 59`. If it evaluates to true, the null statement executes, which means your program does nothing. Then the next statement, `seniorDeal = 0.00;` executes because it is the next statement following the `if` statement. This does not cause a logic error in your program, but think about what happens when the expression in the `if` statement evaluates to false. If false, the null statement does not execute, but the statement `seniorDeal = 0.00;` will execute because it is the next statement after the `if` statement.

Try running the Grandma Discount program with the semicolon in the wrong place. What happens? You should see that even though grandma is old enough to get a $20.00 senior deal, the program will tell you that she gets 0.00. Grandma will not be happy with this program!

 Here's another example. The following code uses an `if` statement along with the equality operator (==) to see if two strings are equal.

```
var firstName = "Tim";
var career = "Teacher";
if(firstName == "Tim")
    console.log("You are a " + career);
```

In this example, if the value of the variable named `firstName` and the string "Tim" are the same, the expression is true, and the statement

```
console.log("You are a " + career);
```

executes. If the expression evaluates to false, the statement

```
console.log("You are a " + career);
```

does not execute.

 Can you use what you have learned about writing `if` statements to study the JavaScript code that follows and then answer the questions?

 When you are finished answering the questions, find the special symbols, keywords, variable names, strings, numbers, operators and methods, then use the chart to color what you find.

You can also color this example on your mobile device using the QR code on the right or by visiting https://www.colormycode.com/colormycode/ex15.html

Orange	Red	Blue	Gray	Light Green	Purple	Pink
Special Symbol	Keyword	Variable Name	String	Operator	Number	Method

```
var myAge = 12;
var OK = "Yes";
var pg13Age = 13;
if(myAge < pg13Age)
    OK = "No";
console.log("My Age: " + myAge);
console.log("OK to see PG13 movies: " + OK);
```

1. What is the exact output when this program executes?

   _____

   _____

2. What is the exact output if the variable named OK is initialized
   with the value "No" rather than the value "Yes"?

   _____

   _____.

3. What is the exact output if the value of myAge is changed to 17?

   _____

   _____

4. What is the exact output if the expression in the if statement is
   changed to myAge <= pg13Age ?

   _____

   _____

Here is another kind of decision statement. It's called the `if-else` statement. It's a two-path decision statement which means that your program will now be able to take one of two paths as a result of evaluating an expression.

 Did you ask yourself whether the word "`else`" is also a keyword? The answer is YES. You now know five JavaScript keywords: `var`, `true`, `false`, `if`, and `else`.

Here is the syntax for writing an `if-else` statement in JavaScript.

```
if(expression)
    statementA;
else
    statementB;
```

 Again, do not include a semicolon at the end of the line containing the keyword `if` and the expression to be tested, or on the line with the keyword `else`. It is allowed but it could create a logic error.

IT WORKS LIKE THIS

An `if-else` statement works like this. The expression in the parentheses is evaluated. If it's true, then *statement A is executed.* Else, if the expression in parentheses is false, then *statementB* is executed. It doesn't matter which path is taken in the program, the statement following the `if-else` statement is the next one to execute.

 Do you remember what a block statement is? Why is this important? Because both *statementA* and *statementB* can be simple statements or block statements.

example Here is an example of some JavaScript code that uses an `if else` statement. Let's call it the Larger or Smaller program.

```
1  var num1 = 11;
2  var num2 = 16;
3  var larger;
4  var smaller;
5  if(num1 > num2)
6  {
7     larger = num1;
8     smaller = num2;
9  }
10 else
11 {
12    larger = num2;
13    smaller = num1;
14 }
15 console.log(larger + " is larger than " + smaller + ".");
```

66

In the Larger or Smaller program, the value of the variable named num1 is tested to see if it is greater than the value of the variable named num2.

You use the greater than operator (>) to make the comparison on line 5. If the expression num1 > num2 evaluates to true, then num1 is larger than num2 and the block statement on lines 6 through 9 executes. This first block statement contains a statement that assigns the value of num1 to the variable named larger, and another statement that assigns the value of num2 to the variable named smaller.

If the expression num1 > num2 evaluates to false, then a different path is followed, and the second block statement on lines 11 to 14 following the keyword else executes. This block statement contains a statement that assigns the value of num2 to the variable named larger, and another statement that assigns the value of num1 to the variable named smaller.

It doesn't matter which path is taken, the next statement to execute is the output statement on line 15.

Open the JavaScript console, type the Larger or Smaller program, then run it. This is what you should see when you run the program.

16 is larger than 11.

Now, change the value of num1 to 25 and run the program again. This is what you should see.

25 is larger than 16.

Now, in the Larger or Smaller program, find the special symbols, keywords, variable names, strings, numbers, operators and methods, and use the chart to color what you find.

You can also color this example on your mobile device using the QR code on the left or by visiting https://www.colormycode.com/colormycode/ex16.html

Orange	Red	Blue	Gray	Light Green	Purple	Pink
Special Symbol	Keyword	Variable Name	String	Operator	Number	Method

```
1  var num1 = 11;
2  var num2 = 16;
3  var larger;
4  var smaller;
5  if(num1 > num2)
6  {
7     larger = num1;
8     smaller = num2;
9  }
10 else
11 {
12    larger = num2;
13    smaller = num1;
14 }
15 console.log(larger + " is larger than " + smaller + ".");
```

Can you use what you have learned about writing `if else` statements to study the JavaScript code that follows and then answer the questions?

 When you are finished answering the questions, find the special symbols, keywords, variable names, strings, numbers, operators and methods, and use the chart to color what you find.

You can also color this example on your mobile device using the QR code on the right or by visiting https://www.colormycode.com/colormycode/ex17.html

Orange	Red	Blue	Gray	Light Green	Purple	Pink
Special Symbol	Keyword	Variable Name	String	Operator	Number	Method

This program was written for a Pokèmon Go player. It is used to figure out how many more items can be placed in the player's bag.

```javascript
var myBagSize;
var itemsInMyBag;
var itemsAvailable;

myBagSize = 600;
itemsInMyBag = 516;

if(myBagSize > itemsInMyBag)
{
   itemsAvailable = myBagSize - itemsInMyBag;
   console.log(itemsAvailable + " items to use.");
}
else
   console.log("Your bag is full.");
```

69

1. What is the exact output when this program executes?

   _____

   _____

2. What is the exact output if the value of `itemsInMyBag` is changed to 601?

   _____

   _____

3. What is the exact output if the variable named `myBagSize` is assigned the value 400 rather than the value 600?

   _____

   _____

There is even more you can do with decision statements in a JavaScript program.

You can nest `if` statements to create more than two paths in a program. When you nest `if` statements, you include an `if` statement within another `if` statement. This is important in programs that need more than two possible paths.

Here is the syntax for writing a nested `if` statement in JavaScript.

```
if(expressionA)
    statementA;
else if(expressionB)
    statementB;
else
    statementC;
```

This is called a nested `if` statement because the second `if` statement is included as part of the first `if` statement.

This is how a nested `if` statement works. If *expressionA* evaluates to true, then *statement A* executes. If *expressionA* evaluates to false, then the computer evaluates *expressionB*. If *expressionB* evaluates to true, then *statement B* executes. If both *expressionA* and *expressionB* evaluate to false, then *statement C* executes. Regardless of which path is taken in this code, the statement following the nested `if-else-if` statement is the next one to execute.

 Here is an example of JavaScript code that includes a nested `if` statement. Let's call it the Teacher Name program.

```
var stuID = 327;
var teacherName;
if(stuID <= 200)
    teacherName = "Jones";
else if(stuID <= 400)
    teacherName = "Hayes";
else
    teacherName = "Miller";
console.log("Teacher: " + teacherName);
```

When you read the preceding code, you can assume that a student ID number is never less than 1 and that a student is assigned to a teacher based on their student ID number.

71

If the value of the variable named stuID is less than or equal to the value 200 (in the range of values from 1 to 200), then the value "Jones" is assigned to the variable named teacherName.

If the value of stuID is not less than or equal to 200, but it is less than or equal to 400 (in the range of values from 201 to 400), then the value "Hayes" is assigned to the variable named teacherName.

If the value of stuID is not in the range of values from 1 to 400, then the value "Miller" is assigned to the variable named teacherName.

As you can see, there are three possible paths this program could take. Regardless of which path the program takes, the next statement to execute is the output statement

```
console.log("Teacher: " + teacherName);
```

In this example, the value of stuID is 327, so when the first comparison (stuID <= 200) is made the result is false. Then the second comparison (stuID <= 400) is made and the result is true so the value "Hayes" is assigned to the variable named teacherName. The else portion is never reached so the output from this program is:

```
Teacher: Hayes
```

Open the JavaScript console, type the Teacher Name program, then run it. This is what you should see when you run the program.

```
Teacher: Hayes
```

Now, change the value of `stuID` to 79 and run the program again. This is what you should see.

```
Teacher: Jones
```

Change the value of `stuID` to 500. Run the program again. This is what you should see.

```
Teacher: Miller
```

 Now, in the Teacher Name program, find the special symbols, keywords, variable names, strings, numbers, operators and methods, and use the chart to color what you find.

You can also color this example on your mobile device using the QR code on the right or by visiting https://www.colormycode.com/colormycode/ex18.html

Orange	Red	Blue	Gray	Light Green	Purple	Pink
Special Symbol	Keyword	Variable Name	String	Operator	Number	Method

```javascript
var stuID = 327;
var teacherName;
if(stuID <= 200)
    teacherName = "Jones";
else if(stuID <= 400)
    teacherName = "Hayes";
else
    teacherName = "Miller";
console.log("Teacher: " + teacherName);
```

73

1. Open the JavaScript console.

2. Type the code shown below after the blinking cursor.

DO NOT PRESS the Enter key after each line. For programs that are more than one line of code, press SHIFT+ENTER to add another line. When all the lines are typed, press the ENTER key to run the program.

```javascript
var largest;
var smallest;
var firstNumber = -50;
var secondNumber = 53;
var thirdNumber = 78;
largest = firstNumber;
if(secondNumber > largest)
    largest = secondNumber;
if(thirdNumber > largest)
    largest = thirdNumber;
smallest = firstNumber;
if(secondNumber < smallest)
    smallest = secondNumber;
if(thirdNumber < smallest)
    smallest = thirdNumber;
console.log("The largest value is " + largest);
console.log("The smallest value is " + smallest);
```

3. Check your typing. Be sure it is exactly the same as what you see in Step 2.

4. This is what you should see when you press the Enter Key to run the program.

```
The largest value is 78
The smallest value is -50
```

5. If you don't see this, you have typed something incorrectly or your statements are not in the correct order. Check and correct your typing and try again. Be sure that you have typed every letter and symbol correctly.

 In the JavaScript code that follows, find the special symbols, keywords, variable names, strings, numbers, operators and methods, and use the chart to color what you find.

You can also color this example on your mobile device using the QR code on the right or by visiting https://www.colormycode.com/colormycode/ex19.html

Orange	Red	Blue	Gray	Light Green	Purple	Pink
Special Symbol	Keyword	Variable Name	String	Operator	Number	Method

```
var largest;
var smallest;
var firstNumber = -50;
var secondNumber = 53;
var thirdNumber = 78;

largest = firstNumber;
if(secondNumber > largest)
     largest = secondNumber;
if(thirdNumber > largest)
     largest = thirdNumber;
smallest = firstNumber;
if(secondNumber < smallest)
     smallest = secondNumber;
if(thirdNumber < smallest)
     smallest = thirdNumber;
console.log("The largest value is " + largest);
console.log("The smallest value is " + smallest);
```

2

Practice Number

1 Open the JavaScript console.

2 Remember flowcharts? Here is a flowchart for a program that tries to guess your lucky number.

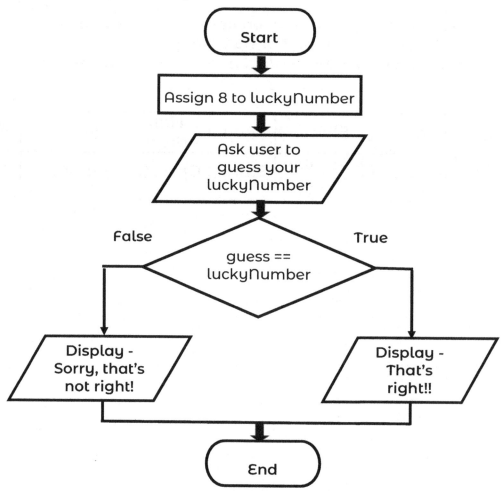

76

3   Here is the JavaScript code that was written using the steps listed in the flowchart to guess a lucky number. Type the code shown below after the blinking cursor. This code checks to see if a user has guessed your lucky number.

DO NOT PRESS the Enter key after each line. For programs that are more than one line of code, press SHIFT+ENTER to add another line. When all the lines are typed, press the ENTER key to run the program.

```javascript
var luckyNumber = 8;
var guess = prompt("Try to guess my lucky number!");
guess = Number(guess);
if(guess == luckyNumber)
{
      alert("That's right!!");
}
else
{
      alert("Sorry. That's not right!");
}
```

4   Check your typing. Be sure it is exactly the same as what you see in Step 3.
5   Press the Enter Key to run the program. If you enter the number 10 as your guess, this is what you should see when you run the program.

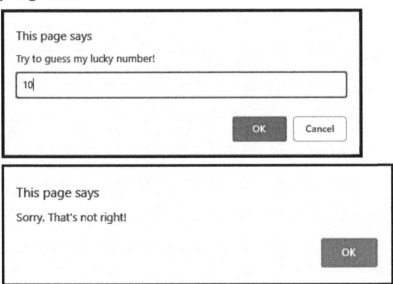

6   Run the program several more times, each time guessing a different number. What do you see when you guess the correct number?

In the JavaScript code that follows, find the special symbols, keywords, variable names, strings, numbers, operators and methods ,and use the chart to color what you find.

You can also color this example on your mobile device using the QR code on the left or by visiting https://www.colormycode.com/colormycode/ex20.html

Orange	Red	Blue	Gray	Light Green	Purple	Pink
Special Symbol	Keyword	Variable Name	String	Operator	Number	Method

```
var luckyNumber = 8;
var guess = prompt("Try to guess my lucky number!");
if(guess == luckyNumber)
{
      alert("That's right!!");
}
else
{
      alert("Sorry. That's not right!");
}
```

3

Practice Number

1 Open the JavaScript console.

2 Type the code shown below after the blinking cursor. This code assigns a letter grade based on a numerical grade, e.g. a grade of 92 would be assigned an "A" and a grade of 52 would be assigned a grade of "F".

 DO NOT PRESS the Enter key after each line. For programs that are more than one line of code, press SHIFT+ENTER to add another line. When all the lines are typed, press the ENTER key to run the program.

```
var grade = 82;
var letterGrade;
if(grade >= 90)
    letterGrade = "A";
else if(grade >= 80)
    letterGrade = "B";
else if(grade >= 70)
    letterGrade = "C";
else if (grade >= 60)
    letterGrade = "D";
else
    letterGrade = "F";
console.log("Your numerical grade is " + grade + ".");
console.log("Your letter grade is " + letterGrade + ".");
```

3 Check your typing. Be sure it is exactly the same as what you see in Step 2.

4 Press the Enter Key to run the program.

5. This is what you should see below the lines that you typed. If you don't see this, you have typed something incorrectly. Check and correct your typing and try again. Be sure that you have typed every letter and symbol correctly.

```
Your numerical grade is 82.
Your letter grade is B.
```

6. Change the grade value to 95, then run the program again. Does the output change?

  In the JavaScript code that follows, find the special symbols, keywords, variable names, strings, numbers, operators and methods, and use the chart to color what you find.

You can also color this example on your mobile device using the QR code on the left or by visiting https://www.colormycode.com/colormycode/ex21.html

Orange	Red	Blue	Gray	Light Green	Purple	Pink
Special Symbol	Keyword	Variable Name	String	Operator	Number	Method

```javascript
var grade = 82;
var letterGrade;
if (grade >= 90)
    letterGrade = "A";
else if(grade >= 80)
    letterGrade = "B";
else if(grade >= 70)
    letterGrade = "C";
else if (grade >= 60)
    letterGrade = "D";
else
    letterGrade = "F";
console.log("Your numerical grade is " + grade + ".");
console.log("Your letter grade is " + letterGrade + ".");
```

It's time for another challenge to write a JavaScript program "from scratch." Here is the description of the program.

Write a JavaScript program that asks your user to enter their name and their favorite color. If they choose the color "red" display their name followed by "I like red too.". If they choose "blue" display their name followed by "Blue is my second favorite color.". If they choose something other than "red" or "blue", display their name and their favorite color.

 Here's a hint. Think about how many paths your program needs to provide. Also, you can use the `prompt()` and `alert()` methods more than once.

Before you begin to write your code, draw a flowchart here.

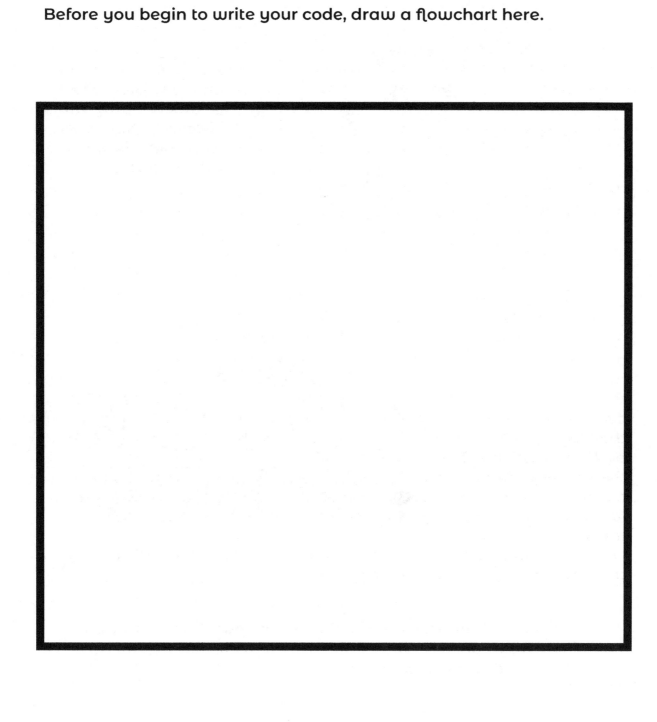

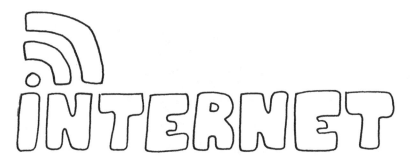

INTERNET

 What do you do if you want the user of your JavaScript program to be able to run the program on the Internet? Before you answer that question, let's answer this one – What is the Internet?

Here is a definition. The Internet is a collection of computer networks from all over the world. It's a network of networks that allows users at any one computer to get information from any other computer and even talk to users at other computers.

 Do you know that what most of us think of as the Internet is really something called the World Wide Web? What's the World Wide Web?

The World Wide Web is only part of the Internet. It is that part that contains web sites and web pages. To create web sites and web pages, developers use HTML. HTML is known as the language of the World Wide Web.

 Here's one more question! What is HTML?

HTML stands for Hypertext Markup Language. HTML is used to mark and describe text, pictures and even JavaScript programs, so a web browser can show them on your screen. Web pages are usually viewed in a web browser like Chrome or Firefox.

Now, let's get to work and learn a little HTML so you can put your JavaScript programs on the World Wide Web.

HTML uses something called tags to format what is displayed on a web page. These tags are words that define how your web browser must format and display the content of a web page. Here are a few things you need to know about HTML and HTML tags:

 You need to write your HTML documents using a text editor like Notepad, Notepad++ , TextEdit or Gedit. These are free. Notepad is included as part of Windows. Notepad++ must be downloaded and installed on your Windows system. TextEdit is included as part of the Macs OS. Gedit is a cross platform text editor which means it can be used on Windows, Mac OS or Linux. It must be downloaded and installed.

 HTML tags are put between angle brackets like this <tag>.

 Except for a few tags, most of the tags have a closing tag that must be included like this </tag>.

There are 5 HTML tags you should know about before you can put your JavaScript program on the World Wide Web.

`<html>` and `</html>` – beginning and ending tags that tell the browser this is an HTML file. You begin and end your HTML file with these tags. Here is what it looks like in the HTML file you will create.

```
<html>


</html>
```

`<head>` and `</head>` - This is where you put general information about the file, like the author, copyright, keywords and/or a description of what appears on the page.

`<title>` and `</title>` - **These tags are placed inside the** `<head>` **tags and provide the title of the web page. You will see this title on the web browser tab.**

Here is what it looks like in the HTML file you will create.

```
<html>
<head>
<title> My First HTML document
</title>
</head>
</html>
```

And, here is what it looks like displayed in a web browser like Chrome.

Your title is shown on the browser tab.

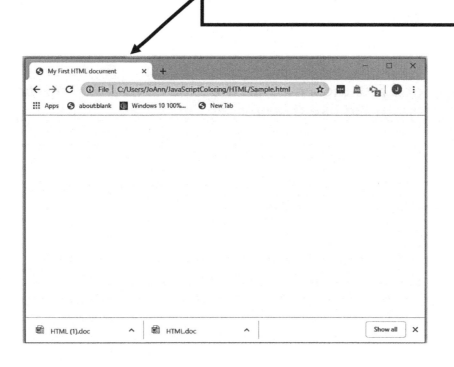

`<body>` and `</body>` - **contain the main content of your web page**

`<script>` and `</script>` - **JavaScript code is inserted between these**

tags.

 This example shows the contents of an html file that includes a short JavaScript program inserted between the `<script>` tags.

```
<html>
<head>
<title> My First HTML document
</title>
</head>
<body>
<script>
     alert("I put my first JavaScript on the Web!!" );
     alert("This program prints your name.");
     var firstName;
     var lastName;
     var fullName;
     firstName = prompt("Enter your first name: ");
     lastName = prompt("Enter your last name: ");
     fullName = firstName + " " + lastName;
     alert("Your name is " + fullName);
     alert("Bye Bye");
</script>
</body>
</html>
```

1. **Open Notepad, or the text editor that you are using, then type the HTML you see below.**

```html
<html>
<head>
<title> My First HTML document
</title>
</head>
<body>
<script>
      alert("I put my first JavaScript on the Web!!" );
      alert("This program prints your name.");
      var firstName;
      var lastName;
      var fullName;
      firstName = prompt("Enter your first name: ");
      lastName = prompt("Enter your last name: ");
      fullName = firstName + " " + lastName;
      alert("Your name is " + fullName);
      alert("Bye Bye");
</script>
</body>
</html>
```

88

2. Save the Notepad file – call it Sample.html

3. Open Chrome or Firefox, type Control-O (Windows) or Command -O (Mac), then open the Sample.html file.

   This is what you should see.

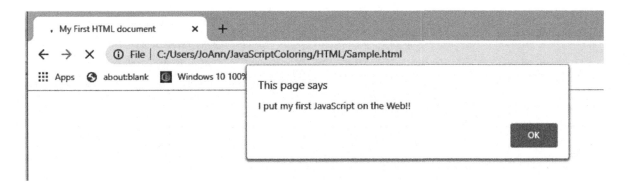

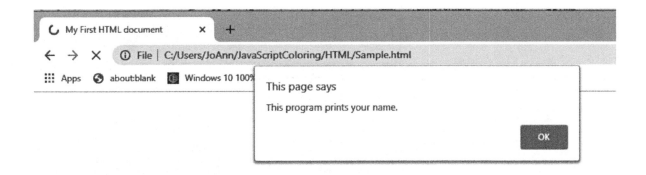

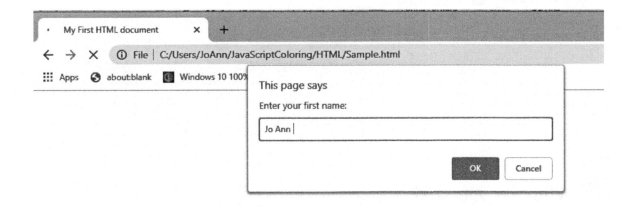

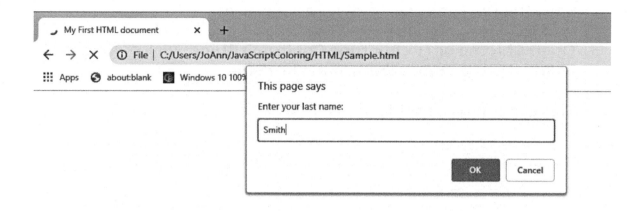

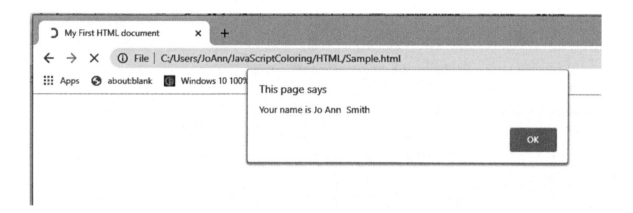

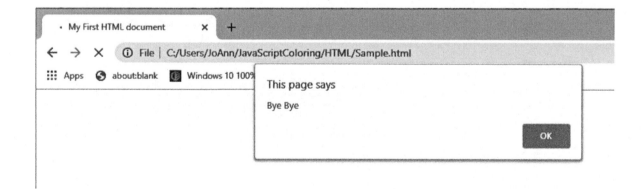

 **What do you see?**

90

I have to think about it!!

In the next section, you'll learn to write JavaScript programs that use loops that will let your program perform actions over and over without having to write the code over and over. You will use the Decision symbol in your flowcharts for this type of program. You learned about the Decision symbol in a previous section.

Here is the Decision symbol.

PULLING (IT) ALL TOGETHER

Let's draw a flowchart to solve the following: You need to write a program that allows you to keep track of how many people in your class are right handed and how many are left handed. You think about this problem for a while and figure out that all you have to do is find out how many people are in your class, ask if they are right handed or left handed and keep track of how many are right handed and how many are left handed.

91

But, how can you do this in a program? You will have to ask how many people are in your class and you will also have to ask many times if the person is left or right handed. Each time you ask the right handed/left handed question, you will add 1 to a counter that keeps track of left handed persons or a different counter that keeps track of right handed persons.

You also realize that you can use a decision statement to figure out if the person is left or right handed and another decision to know when you have asked about each person in your class.

Let's see what a flowchart would look like to solve the Left/Right problem. It's on the next page.

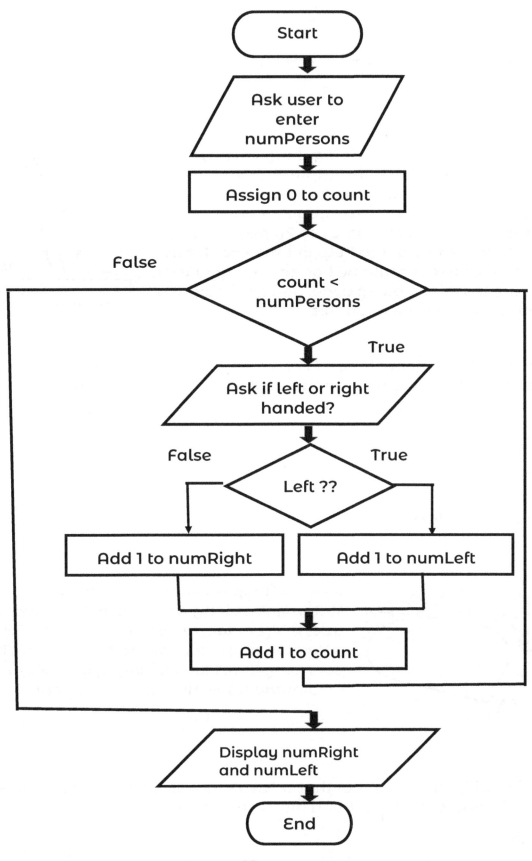

93

LOOPS

Computers are good at doing things that are boring for humans. For example, let's say your basketball coach has asked you to help calculate a shooting percentage for each member of the team. There are 20 people on your team. You want to help out the coach but this sounds like it could be boring. But, now that you are learning how to code, you could write a JavaScript program to do this.

First, let's learn about loops. *Loops* offer a quick and easy way to do something over and over. In this section, you will learn about two different kinds of loops:

 While **Loops**

 For **Loops**

A `while` loop repeats a statement or a block statement as long as an expression evaluates to true. A `while` loop is written to repeat for an unknown number of times. Often, something in your program, like user input, will determine how many times the loop will repeat.

 Did you remember that a JavaScript statement can be either a simple statement or a block statement?

94

A block statement is made up of more than one JavaScript statement. To make a block statement in JavaScript you have to put the statements inside a pair of special symbols called curly braces.

Let's take a look at the syntax, or rules, for writing a `while` loop in JavaScript.

```
while(expression)

{

    statement or block statement;

}
```

You begin with the keyword `while`.

Do you remember that a keyword is a word that has a special meaning for JavaScript? What other keywords have you already learned? If you answered `var`, `true`, `false`, `if` and `else`, you're right.

After you type the keyword `while` to begin a `while` loop, you follow it with an expression placed within parentheses.

When a `while` statement is included in a program, the expression within the parentheses is evaluated. If it is true, then the computer executes the `statement or block statement` included in the loop. It continues to execute the statement or statements as long as the expression within the parentheses continues to evaluate to true. If the expression in parentheses is false, then the computer does not execute the `statement or block statement`.

example Here's an example of a program that uses a `while` loop with a block statement.

```
var howMany = prompt("How many times do you want to repeat
the loop?");
var loops = 0;
howMany = Number(howMany);
while(loops < howMany)
{
    console.log("JavaScript Programming is fun. " + loops);
    loops = loops + 1;
}
console.log("Done");
```

When this program is run, this is what you see.

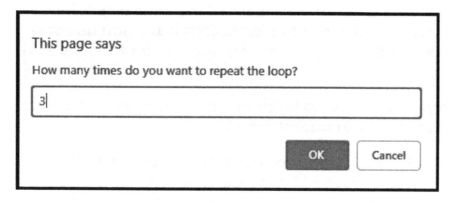

```
JavaScript Programming is fun. 0
JavaScript Programming is fun. 1
JavaScript Programming is fun. 2
Done
```

Notice that a block statement is used in this example because more than one statement needs to be executed.

The first statement in the loop causes the text "JavaScript Programming is fun." along the value of `loops` to appear on the user's screen. The second statement, `loops = loops + 1;`, is important because it causes the value of `loops` to be increased by one. The variable named `loops` is called the loop control variable because its value controls whether the loop executes or not.

When the loop is first encountered, the comparison, `loops < howMany`, is made for the first time when the value of `loops` is 0. The 0 is compared to, and found to be less than the value of `howMany` whose value is 3. This means the condition is true, and the text "JavaScript Programming is fun. " along with a 0 is displayed.

 Did you remember that `Number()` is used to change a string to a number?

The next statement, `loops = loops + 1;`, causes 1 to be added to the value of `loops`. The second time the comparison is made, the value of `loops` is 1, which is still less than 3. This causes the text to appear a second time along with a 1, followed by adding 1 to the value of `loops`. The third comparison also results in a true value because the value of `loops` is now 2, and 2 is still less than 3. This results in the text appearing a third time along with a 2. Then 1 is added to the value of `loops` again. The fourth time the comparison is made, the value of `loops` is 3, which is not less than 3. This causes the program to exit the loop.

 Look at the beginning of the `while` loop – `while(loops < howMany)` and notice that there is no semicolon after the ending parenthesis. Placing a semicolon after the ending parenthesis is NOT a syntax error, but it is a logic error.

 Placing a semicolon after the ending parenthesis results in an infinite loop, which is a loop that never stops executing. It never stops executing because the semicolon is a statement called the null statement and is interpreted as "do nothing." Think of a `while` loop with a semicolon after the ending parenthesis as meaning "while the condition is true, do NOTHING forever".

When you use a `while` loop in your JavaScript programs, be sure you follow these rules.

 You must initialize a loop control variable. This variable will control the loop. For example, `var loops = 0;`

 You must compare the loop control variable to a value to decide whether the loop continues or stops. This comparison always results in a true or false value. For example, the comparison `while (loops < howMany)` results in a true or false value.

 Within the loop, you must change the value of the loop control variable. For example, `loops = loops + 1;`

Use what you have learned about writing `while` loops to study the JavaScript code that follows, then answer the questions.

 When you are finished answering the questions, find the special symbols, keywords, variable names, strings, operators, numbers and methods, and then use the chart to color what you find.

 You can also color this example on your mobile device using the QR code on the left or by visiting https://www.colormycode.com/colormycode/ex22.html

Orange	Red	Blue	Gray	Light Green	Purple	Pink
Special Symbol	Keyword	Variable Name	String	Operator	Number	Method

```
var numberOfTimes = 1;
while(numberOfTimes < 5)
{
    console.log("Value of numberOfTimes is " + numberOfTimes);
    numberOfTimes = numberOfTimes + 1;
}
```

1. What is the loop control variable?

   _____

2. What is the output?

   _____

3. What is the output if the code is changed to
   ```
   while(numberOfTimes <= 5)?
   ```

   _____

A `for` loop also repeats a statement or a block statement as long as an expression evaluates to true. A `for` loop is written to repeat a known number of times.

Here is the syntax for writing a `for` loop.

```
for(expression1; expression2; expression3)
    statement or block statement;
```

In JavaScript, the `for` loop is made up of three expressions that are separated by semicolons and placed within parentheses. This is how the `for` loop works.

- The first time the `for` loop is encountered `expression1` is evaluated. Usually, this expression initializes a variable that is used to control the `for` loop.
- Next, `expression2` is evaluated. If `expression2` evaluates to true, the statement or block statement executes. If `expression2` evaluates to false, the loop is exited.
- After the loop statement or block statement executes `expression3` is evaluated. The third expression usually changes the value of the loop control variable that was initialized in `expression1`.
- After `expression3` is evaluated, `expression2` is evaluated again. If `expression2` still evaluates to true, the loop statement or block statement executes again, and then `expression3` is evaluated again.
- This continues until `expression2` evaluates to false.

example Here is an example of a `for` loop that includes a block statement written in JavaScript.

```
var total = 0;
var counter;
var numTimes = 7;
for(counter = 0; counter < numTimes; counter = counter + 1)
{
    total = total + counter;
    console.log("Value of total is: " + total);
}
```

In this `for` loop, the variable named `counter` is initialized to 0 in the first expression. The second expression is a comparison that evaluates to true or false. When the expression `counter < numTimes` is evaluated the first time, the value of `counter` is 0 and the result is true. The loop body is then entered. This is where a new value is determined and assigned to the variable named `total` and then is displayed. The first time through the loop, the output is as follows:
`Value of total is: 0.`

After the output is displayed, the third expression in the `for` loop is evaluated. This adds 1 to the value of `counter`, making the new value of `counter` equal to 1. When the second expression is evaluated a second time, the value of `counter` is 1. The program then tests to see if the value of `counter` is less than `numTimes`. This results in a true value and causes the loop body to execute again where a new value is computed for `total` and then displayed. The second time through the loop, the output is as follows: `Value of total is: 1.`

Next, the third expression is evaluated. This adds 1 to the value of `counter`. The value of `counter` is now 2. The second expression is evaluated a third time and again is true because 2 is less than `numTimes`. The third time through, the loop body changes the value of `total` to 3 because the value of `total` is 1 and the value of `counter` is 2. Therefore 1 + 2 is 3. The new value of `total` is then displayed. The output is as follows:
`Value of total is: 3.`

This process continues until the value of `counter` becomes 7. At this time, 7 is not less than `numTimes`, so the second expression is false, and causes an exit from the `for` loop.

Here is the output when this program is run.

```
Value of numValue is: 0
Value of numValue is: 1
Value of numValue is: 3
Value of numValue is: 6
Value of numValue is: 10
Value of numValue is: 15
Value of numValue is: 21
```

Use what you have learned about writing `for` loops to study the JavaScript code , then answer the questions that follow.

 When you are finished answering the questions, find the special symbols, keywords, variable names, strings, operators, numbers and methods, then use the chart to color what you find.

You can also color this example on your mobile device using the QR code on the right or by visiting https://www.colormycode.com/colormycode/ex23.html

Orange	Red	Blue	Gray	Light Green	Purple	Pink
Special Symbol	Keyword	Variable Name	String	Operator	Number	Method

```
var howMany = 12;
var numLoops;
for(numLoops = 1; numLoops <= howMany; numLoops = numLoops + 1)
{
    console.log("Value of numLoops is: " + numLoops);
    numLoops = numLoops + 1;
}
```

Answer the following three questions with "True" or "False."

1. This loop executes 12 times. Think hard. This is tricky!

    _____

2. Changing the $<=$ operator to $<$ will make no difference in the output.

    _____

3. This loop executes 6 times. Think hard. This is tricky!

    _____

Finding an Average

Now that you are learning JavaScript, many people want your help. Your science teacher has asked you to write a program that she can use to calculate an average score for a test she gave last week.

Here's what you need to know about how to find the average test score. All you have to do is add all the students' test scores, and then divide that sum by the number of students who took the test.

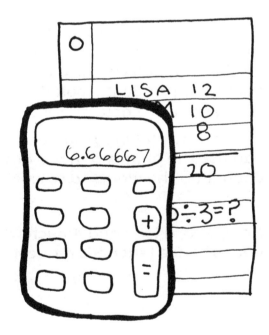

Let's start thinking about this problem. It doesn't take too long to realize that you better ask your teacher a question – like how many students took the test? Her answer – that depends on how many students are in class the day the test is given. You realize you will have to ask this question each time she uses the program.

OK, back to thinking. To solve this problem you will have to get a test score and then add that value to a total. You realize you will have to do this over and over until there are no test scores left. AHA! The words "over and over" are a big clue here. Sounds like a loop to me.

Once you get all of the test scores and figure out the sum of all the test scores, you divide that sum by the number of students to find the average.

So the problem is solved and you can just start writing your JavaScript now. Right? Think about it. You've got a few more things to figure out. Such as, how do you get the test scores? And, how will you know how many test scores there are? That's important because you need that value to find the average.

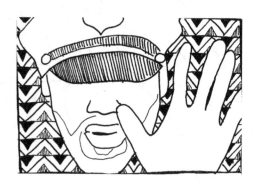

Now that you know about the `prompt()` method, you can use that method to ask the user of your program to enter the test scores. You realize that you can also use the `prompt()` method to ask the user how many students took the test. Wow, that `prompt()` method is really good to know about.

This is a helpful program for your science teacher. Why? Because she can use the program many times using a different number of students each time she wants to calculate an average for a test.

Now, take a look at a flowchart that shows how you intend to solve your science teacher's request to find the average test score.

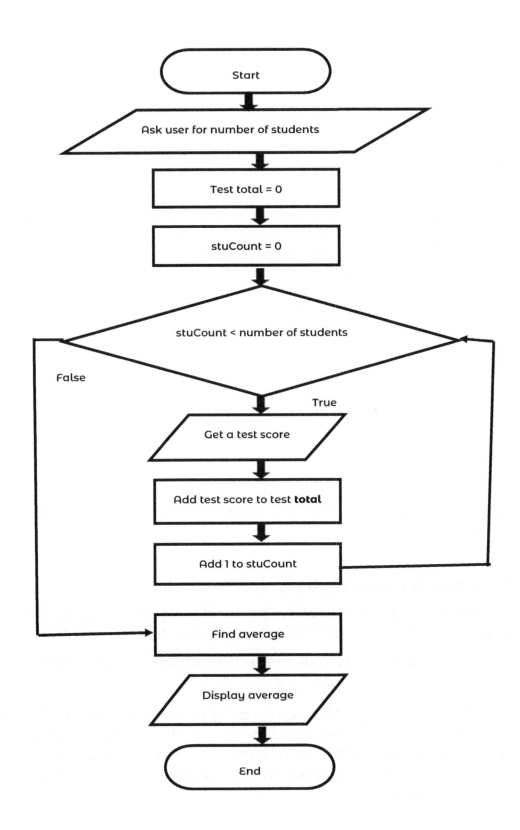

The following JavaScript code is written using the flowchart as a guide. Notice that it includes a `for` loop on lines 9 through 13.

```
1  var numStudents;
2  var stuCount;
3  var testScore;
4  var testTotal;
5  var average;
6  numStudents = prompt("Enter number of students: ");
7  numStudents = Number(numStudents);
8  testTotal = 0;
9  for(stuCount = 0; stuCount < numStudents; stuCount =
   stuCount + 1)
10 {
11      testScore = prompt("Enter student's score: ");
12      testTotal = testTotal + Number(testScore);
13 }
14 average = testTotal / numStudents;
15 alert("The average is: " + average);
```

Notice that line 12 in the loop body includes what is called an accumulator,

```
testTotal = testTotal + Number(testScore);.
```

That is how the total of all test scores is calculated.

Also, notice that the `Number()` method is used to change the string value of `numStudents` to a number on line 7 before the loop is entered.

Did you notice that the statement that calculates the average,

```
average = testTotal / numStudents;
```

is outside of the loop? You really only want to do this once in your program – after all of the test scores have been entered and included in the total. If you put the average calculation inside the loop, the average would be calculated each time the loop executes. That is not necessary, right?

What happens if a user enters a 0 when asked to enter the number of students? You'd be right if you answered the `for` loop would not execute because the value of `numStudents` is 0 and the value of `stuCount` is also 0.

Here's a few more things to know about accumulating totals. Did you notice that the accumulator, `testTotal`, is initialized to 0 on line 8? If you don't give `testTotal` an initial value, it will contain an unknown value. This value is referred to as a "garbage" value. Not only will `testTotal` contain a garbage value, your program will be "garbage" too because you won't get the correct results.

Let's play computer and walk through this code one line at a time to be sure you understand what is happening.

After you declare the variables, `numStudents`, `stuCount`, `testScore`, `testTotal`, and `average` on lines 1 through 5, the `prompt()` method is used on line 6 to ask the user to enter the number of students who took the test. This value is assigned to the variable named `numStudents`.

On line 7, the variable named `numStudents` is converted to a number using the `Number()` method and assigned right back to the variable named `numStudents`.

Remember that the value stored in `numStudents` has to be changed to a number, e.g. `numStudents = Number (numStudents);`. Do you remember why? The answer is the `prompt()` method always treats user input as a string. To make a comparison with another number in this program, the string values must be changed to numbers.

The accumulator `testTotal` is initialized with the value 0 on line 8.

On line 9, you see a `for` loop. A `for` loop is a good choice because, at this point in the program, you know the loop should execute as many times as there are students who took the test. You use the `for` loop's first expression to initialize `stuCount` with a 0, and then the second expression is evaluated to see if `stuCount` is less than `numStudents`. If this is true, the body of the loop executes, using the `prompt()` method on line 11, this time asking the user to enter a test score.

 Did you remember that the value stored in `testScore` must be changed to a number? Why? So your program can do arithmetic.

Next, on line 12, the value of `testScore`, which is now a number, is added to the accumulator, `testTotal = testTotal + testScore;`.

Back to the top of the loop found on line 9 of the program, where 1 is added to `stuCount`, like this, `stuCount = stuCount + 1`. The new value of `stuCount` is then tested to see if it is less than `numStudents`. If this is true again, the loop executes a second time. The loop continues to execute until the value of `stuCount < numStudents` is false. Outside the `for` loop on line 14, the program calculates the average test score by dividing `testTotal` by `stuCount`.

 In the JavaScript code that follows, find the special symbols, keywords, variable names, strings, operators, numbers and methods, and use the chart to color what you find.

 You can also color this example on your mobile device using the QR code on the left or by visiting https://www.colormycode.com/colormycode/ex24.html

Orange	Red	Blue	Gray	Light Green	Purple	Pink
Special Symbol	Keyword	Variable Name	String	Operator	Number	Method

```
1  var numStudents;
2  var stuCount;
3  var testScore;
4  var testTotal;
5  var average;
6  numStudents = prompt("Enter number of students: ");
7  numStudents = Number(numStudents);
8  testTotal = 0;
9  for(stuCount = 0; stuCount < numStudents; stuCount =
   stuCount + 1)
10 {
11     testScore = prompt("Enter student's score: ");
12     testTotal = testTotal + Number(testScore);
13 }
14 average = testTotal / numStudents;
15 alert("The average is: " + average);
```

 Can you use what you have learned about finding averages to study the JavaScript code on the next page, then answer the questions?

 When you are finished answering the questions, find the special symbols, keywords, variable names, strings, operators, numbers and methods, and use the chart to color what you find.

You can also color this example on your mobile device using the QR code on the right or by visiting https://www.colormycode.com/colormycode/ex25.html

Orange	Red	Blue	Gray	Light Green	Purple	Pink
Special Symbol	Keyword	Variable Name	String	Operator	Number	Method

```
var count;
var rainAmount;
var sum = 0;
var average;
for(count = 1; count <= 7; count = count + 1)
{
    rainAmount = prompt("Enter rainfall amount for Day " +
count);
    rainAmount = Number(rainAmount);
    alert("Day " + count + "rainfall amount is " +
rainAmount + " inches");
    sum = sum + rainAmount;
}
average = sum / 7;
alert("Average rainfall for the week is: " + average);
```

1. **What do you think would happen when you run this program if the variable named** `sum` **is not initialized with the value 0?**

   _____

2. **Could you replace the 7 in the statement** `average = sum / 7;` **with the variable named** `count` **and still get the correct result? Why?**

   _____

OH SNAP...
THAT'S NOT RIGHT

Here's some news. You cannot depend on the people who use your program to do what you ask them to do, especially when you ask them for input. This is going to be a problem, right? To solve this you'll learn how to validate input. You do this so you can avoid problems caused by input that is not what your program expects or needs.

 Here's an example. If your program asks a user to enter a specific value, let's say a "Y" for "yes" or an "n" for "no", in response to a question, then your program is going to have to check to see that your user really entered a "Y" or "n". You must also decide what your program should do if the user's input is not a "Y" or an "n".

 As an example, take a look at this code:

```
var answer;
answer = prompt("Do you want to continue? Enter Y or N.");
while(answer != "Y" && answer != "N")
{
    answer = prompt("That's not right. Please type Y or N.");
}
```

In the example, the variable named `answer` contains your user's answer to the question "Do you want to continue? Enter Y or N." In the expression that is part of the `while` loop, the program tests to see if your user really did enter "Y" or "N". If not, the program enters the loop and tells the user he or she did not enter correct input and then requests that he or she try again to type "Y" or "N". The expression in the `while` loop is tested again to see if the user entered correct data this time. If not, the loop body executes again and continues to execute until the user finally enters a "Y" or an "N".

 There is something new in this example. It's a new operator. It looks like this, `&&`, and is written as two & symbols with no space between them.

The `&&` operator is called the AND operator that you can use when you want to ask more than one question but get only one answer. Here is how it works.

RULE: All expressions must be true for the entire expression to be true.

Here is how the `while` loop is written in our example.

```
while(answer != "Y" && answer != "N")
```

There are really two questions being asked.

 Is the value of the variable named `answer` not equal to a "Y"?

AND

 Is the value of the variable named `answer` not equal to an "N"?

If the answer to question one is true AND the answer to question 2 is also true, then the result is true and you know that the user did not enter a "Y" or an "N". If either question one is false or question two is false or both are false, then the result is false and you know that you have good input. That is, the user either entered a "Y" or an "N".

 Study the code that follows and find the special symbols, keywords, variable names, strings, operators and methods, and use the chart to color what you find.

You can also color this example on your mobile device using the QR code on the right or by visiting https://www.colormycode.com/colormycode/ex26.html

Orange	Red	Blue	Gray	Light Green	Pink
Special Symbol	Keyword	Variable Name	String	Operator	Method

```
var answer;
answer = prompt("Do you want to continue? Enter Y or N.");
while(answer != "Y" && answer != "N")
{
    answer = prompt("That's not right. Please type Y or N.");
}
```

You can also verify user input in a program that asks a user to enter numbers. For example, your program could ask a user to enter a number in the range of 1 to 10. It is very important to verify this input, especially if your program uses the input in arithmetic calculations. What would happen if the user entered the word "two" instead of the number 2? Or, what would happen if the user entered 500? It is likely that your program would not run correctly.

The following code example shows you how to verify that a user enters correct numbers.

```
var answer;
answer = prompt("Please enter a number between 1 and 10.");
answer = Number(answer);
while(answer < 1 || answer > 10)
{
    answer = prompt("Number must be between 1 and 10. Try
                         again.");
    answer = Number(answer);
}
```

 There is also something new in this example. It's another new operator. It looks like this, ||, and is written as two | symbols with no space between them.

The || operator is called the OR operator that you can use when you want to ask more than one question but get only one answer. Here is how it works.

RULE: At least one expression must be true for the entire expression to be true.

Here is how the while loop is written in our example.

```
while(answer < 1 || answer > 10)
```

There are really two questions being asked.

 Is the value of the variable named answer less than 1?

OR

 Is the value of the variable named answer > 10?

If the answer to question one is true OR the answer to question 2 is true, then the result is true and you know that the user did not enter a number between 1 and 10. They either entered a number that is less than 1 or they entered a number that is greater than 10. In either case, you know that your user has entered a number that is not correct. If either question one is false or question two is false or both are false, then the result is false and you know that you have good input. That is, your user has entered a number between 1 and 10.

 Study the code that follows and find the special symbols, keywords, variable names, strings, operators, numbers and methods, and use the chart to color what you find.

You can also color this example on your mobile device using the QR code on the right or by visiting https://www.colormycode.com/colormycode/ex27.html

Orange	Red	Blue	Gray	Light Green	Purple	Pink
Special Symbol	Keyword	Variable Name	String	Operator	Number	Method

```
var answer;

answer = prompt("Please enter a number between 1 and 10.");

answer = Number(answer);

while(answer < 1 || answer > 10)

{

    answer = prompt("Number must be between 1 and 10. Try again.");

    answer = Number(answer);

}
```

Can you use what you have learned about checking user input to study this JavaScript code and then answer the questions that follow?

1. You plan to use the following statement in a JavaScript program to check user input.

```
while(answer == "")
```

What would your user enter to cause this to be true?

_____

2. You plan to use the following statement in a JavaScript program to check user input.

```
while(answer == "N" || answer == "n")
```

What would a user enter to cause this test to be true?

_____

3. You plan to use the following statement in a JavaScript program to validate user input.

```
while(userAnswer < 50 || userAnswer > 100)
```

What would a user enter to cause this test to be true?

_____

1

Practice One

1. Open the JavaScript console.

2. Type the code shown below after the blinking cursor. This JavaScript program prints the numbers 1 through 10 multiplied by 2 and by 5.

DO NOT PRESS the Enter key after each line. For programs that are more than one line of code, press SHIFT+ENTER to add another line. When all the lines are typed, press the ENTER key to run the program.

```javascript
var number = 1;

var byTwo;

var byFive;

while(number <= 10)
{
    byTwo = number * 2;
    byFive = number * 5;
    console.log(number + " " + byTwo + " " + byFive);
    number = number + 1;
}
console.log("All Done!");
```

3. Check your typing. Be sure it is exactly the same as what you see in Step 2.

4. This is what you should see when you run the program.

```
1  2  5
2  4  10
3  6  15
4  8  20
5  10  25
6  12  30
7  14  35
8  16  40
9  18  45
10  20  50
All Done!
```

5. If you don't see this, you have typed something incorrectly or your statements are not in the correct order. Check and correct your typing and try again. Be sure that you have typed every letter and symbol correctly!

 In the JavaScript code that follows, find the special symbols, keywords, variable names, strings, operators, numbers and methods, and use the chart to color what you find.

 You can also color this example on your mobile device using the QR code on the left or by visiting https://www.colormycode.com/colormycode/ex28.html

Orange	Red	Blue	Gray	Light Green	Purple	Pink
Special Symbol	Keyword	Variable Name	String	Operator	Number	Method

```
var number = 1;
var byTwo;
var byFive;
while(number <= 10)
{
     byTwo = number * 2;
     byFive = number * 5;
     console.log(number + " " + byTwo + " " + byFive);
     number = number + 1;
}
console.log("All Done!");
```

2

Practice Number

1   Open the JavaScript console.

2   Remember flowcharts? Here is a flowchart for a program that prints all the odd numbers from 1 to 20 using a `for` loop.

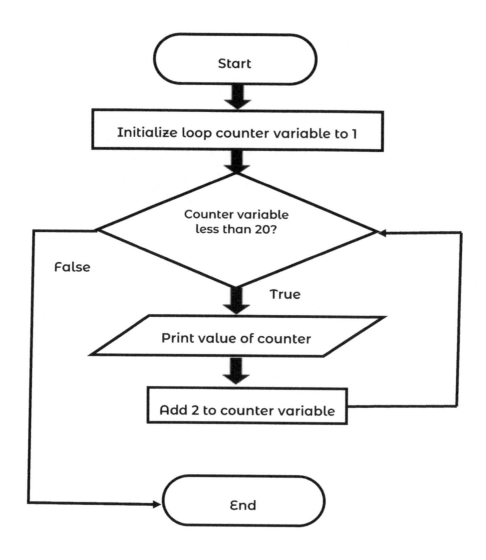

3 And, here is the JavaScript code that was written using the steps listed in the flowchart to print the odd numbers from 1 to 20. Type the code shown below after the blinking cursor.

DO NOT PRESS the Enter key after each line. For programs that are more than one line of code, press SHIFT+ENTER to add another line. When all the lines are typed, press the ENTER key to run the program.

```
var num;
for(num = 1; num <= 20; num = num + 2)
{
        console.log(num + " is an odd number.");
}
```

3. Check your typing. Be sure it is exactly the same as what you see in Step 2.

4. This is what you should see when you run the program.

```
1 is an odd number.

3 is an odd number.

5 is an odd number.

7 is an odd number.

9 is an odd number.

11 is an odd number.

13 is an odd number.

15 is an odd number.

17 is an odd number.

19 is an odd number.
```

5. If you don't see this, you have typed something incorrectly or your statements are not in the correct order. Check and correct your typing and try again. Be sure that you have typed every letter and symbol correctly.

6. Run the program several more times, each time changing the range for the numbers, e.g. change 20 to 50 or change 20 to 10.

 In the JavaScript code that follows, find the special symbols, keywords, variable names, strings, operators, numbers and methods, and use the chart to color what you find.

 You can also color this example on your mobile device using the QR code on the left or by visiting https://www.colormycode.com/colormycode/ex29.html

Orange	Red	Blue	Gray	Light Green	Purple	Pink
Special Symbol	Keyword	Variable Name	String	Operator	Number	Method

```
var num;

for(num = 1; num <= 20; num = num + 2)

{

        console.log(num + " is an odd number.");

}
```

3

Practice Number

1 Open the JavaScript console.

2 Type the code shown below after the blinking cursor. This code allows a user to enter numerical grades for multiple students. It assigns a letter grade based on the numerical grade, e.g. a grade of 92 would be assigned an "A" and a grade of 52 would be assigned a grade of "F".

 DO NOT PRESS the Enter key after each line. For programs that are more than one line of code, press SHIFT+ENTER to add another line. When all the lines are typed, press the ENTER key to run the program.

```javascript
var numGrades;
var count;
var grade;
var letterGrade;
numGrades = prompt("How many grades do you want to enter?");
numGrades = Number(numGrades);
for(count = 0; count < numGrades; count = count + 1)
{
    grade = prompt("Enter a grade: ");
    grade = Number(grade);
    if(grade >= 90)
        letterGrade = "A";
    else if(grade >= 80)
        letterGrade = "B";
    else if(grade >= 70)
        letterGrade = "C";
    else if (grade >= 60)
        letterGrade = "D";
    else
        letterGrade = "F";
    console.log("Your numerical grade is " + grade + ".");
    console.log("Your letter grade is " + letterGrade + ".");
}
```

3. Check your typing. Be sure it is exactly the same as what you see in Step 2.

4. Press the Enter Key to run the program.

5. If you entered 5 grades – 80, 90, 80, 80, and 70, this is what you should see below the lines that you typed. If you don't see this, you have typed something incorrectly. Check and correct your typing and try again. Be sure that you have typed every letter and symbol correctly!

```
Your numerical grade is 80.
Your letter grade is B.
Your numerical grade is 90.
Your letter grade is A.
Your numerical grade is 80.
Your letter grade is B.
Your numerical grade is 80.
Your letter grade is B.
Your numerical grade is 70.
Your letter grade is C.
```

6. Change the grade values and the number of grades. Run the program again.

 Does the output change?

 In the JavaScript code that follows, find the special symbols, keywords, variable names, strings, operators, numbers and methods, and use the chart to color what you find.

 You can also color this example on your mobile device using the QR code on the left or by visiting https://www.colormycode.com/colormycode/ex30.html

Orange	Red	Blue	Gray	Light Green	Purple	Pink
Special Symbol	Keyword	Variable Name	String	Operator	Number	Method

```javascript
var numGrades;
var count;
var grade;
var letterGrade;
numGrades = prompt("How many grades do you want to enter?");
numGrades = Number(numGrades);
for(count = 0; count < numGrades; count = count + 1)
{
    grade = prompt("Enter a grade: ");
    grade = Number(grade);
    if(grade >= 90)
            letterGrade = "A";
    else if(grade >= 80)
                letterGrade = "B";
    else if(grade >= 70)
                letterGrade = "C";
    else if (grade >= 60)
                letterGrade = "D";
    else
                letterGrade = "F";
    console.log("Your numerical grade is " + grade + ".");
    console.log("Your letter grade is " + letterGrade + ".");

}
```

It's time for another challenge to write a JavaScript program "from scratch." Here is the description of the program.

Write a JavaScript program to print multiplication tables. Your program should allow the user to enter a number that represents the multiplication table you want to print. For example, if the user enters 8, then you would print the 8s multiplication table from 1 to 10.

8 * 1 = 8

8 * 2 = 16

8 * 3 = 24

8 * 4 = 32

8 * 5 = 40

8 * 6 = 48

8 * 7 = 56

8 * 8 = 64

8 * 9 = 72

8 * 10 = 80

MULTIPLICATION TABLE

1	2	3	4	5	6	7	8	9	10
2	4	6	8	10	12	14	16	18	20
3	6	9	12	15	18	21	24	27	30
4	8	12	16	20	24	28	32	36	40
5	10	15	20	25	30	35	40	45	50
6	12	18	24	30	36	42	48	54	60
7	14	21	28	35	42	49	56	63	70
8	16	24	32	40	48	56	64	72	80
9	18	27	36	45	54	63	72	81	90
10	20	30	40	50	60	70	80	90	100

Before you begin to write your code, draw a flowchart here.

Glossary

accumulator – a variable used to contain the total of multiple values

alert() – a method that displays a message in a pop-up dialog box along with an OK button

algorithm – a step by step list of directions that must be followed to solve a problem

associativity - the direction (right to left or left to right) in which operations are performed when one or more operators have the same precedence

block statement - allows you to use multiple statements in a JavaScript program where only one statement is expected; a block is created using a pair of curly braces that look like this { }

browser - a computer program providing access to sites on the World Wide Web.

camel case - spelling variable names (that are made up of more than one word) where the first letter of the first word is lower case and the first letter of every other word is upper case

case sensitive - ability to tell the difference between the upper case letters and lower case letters

Chrome – a web browser developed by Google

console - another word for your computer screen

console.log() - a JavaScript method that prints on the screen

curly braces – used to create a block statement

decision statement - allows a program to choose a path in a program

decision symbol – a flowchart symbol that represents a decision or branching point in a program

declaration – giving a variable a name and telling the computer that you will be using the variable in a program

expression – variables combined with operators that result in a value

flowchart – a diagram that shows a step-by-step list of directions that must be followed to solve a problem

flow line – a flowchart symbol that connects other symbols in a flowchart; the flow moves in the direction in which the arrows point

for loop – used in programs to repeat a statement or a block statement multiple times

garbage – an incorrect value stored in a variable

HTML – Hypertext Markup Language - the language of the World Wide Web

if else statement – a two path decision statement that creates two paths your program may take

if statement – a single path decision statement used in programs to decide whether a certain statement or block statement will be executed

infinite loop – a loop that never stops executing

initialize – giving a variable a value when it is declared

input output symbol – a flowchart symbol that indicates receiving information (input) or providing information (output)

interactive input – input provided by a human running a program

Internet - a collection of computer networks all over the world

iteration – perform an action over and over

JavaScript – a programming language

keyword – words that have a special meaning, Examples: `var, true, false, if, else, for, while`

logic error - causes your program to produce incorrect results

loop control variable – a variable used to determine when a loop stops executing

method – code that performs a specific task

nested if statement - an `if` statement that creates more than two paths in a program, an `if` statement within an `if` statement

null statement – a statement that does nothing

Number() - a method that changes a string to a number

operation – an action you want the computer to perform

operator - a symbol that is used to perform an operation

    = assignment - `var firstName = "Jo Ann";`

    + addition - `offset = offset + 60;`

    + concatenation – `newString = "JavaScript" + " Programmer";`

    * multiplication - `offset = offset * 2;`

    / division - `offset = offset / 2;`

    < less than - `if(size < 80)`

    > greater than - `if(size > 0)`

    <= less than or equal to - `if(size <= 80)`

    >= greater than or equal to - `if(size >= 1)`

    == equality - `if(size == 8)`

    != inequality - `if(size != 8)`

    % modulus - `if(value % 2 == 0)`

&& AND - all expressions must be true for the entire expression to be true. Example, `while(answer != "Y" && answer != "N")`

|| OR – only one expression must be true for the entire expression to be true. Example, `while(answer < 1 || answer > 10)`

precedence - the order in which mathematical operations are evaluated

process symbol – a flowchart symbol that indicates something being done

programming language – specific words and rules for instructing a computer to perform specific tasks

prompt() – a method used in JavaScript programs to ask a user for input

sequential statement – statements that the computer runs one after another, in the order in which you write them

special symbol - ; (semicolon), " (quotation mark), (and) (parentheses)

syntax – rules you must follow to write correct JavaScript statements

syntax error – an error that occurs because you have not followed the rules for writing JavaScript statements; programs with syntax errors will not run

tag – used in HTML to specify how web pages are displayed

    <html> and </html> - beginning and ending tags that tell the browser this is an HTML file

    <head> and </head> general information about the file

    <title> and </title) – title of the web page

    <body> and </body> - main content of the web page

    <script> and </script> - JavaScript code

terminal symbol – a flowchart symbol that indicates the beginning point and ending point

text box - a rectangular area on the screen where a user enters text

validate input – check that user input is acceptable

variable – used by programs to store data that can vary as the program runs

while loop – used in programs to repeat a statement or block statement as long as an expression evaluates to true

World Wide Web (www) – the part of the internet that contains web sites and web pages

Made in the USA
Monee, IL
14 December 2019